SUPER
MEETINGS

FOR KIDS GRADES 4-6

VICTOR BOOKS®
A DIVISION OF SCRIPTURE PRESS PUBLICATIONS INC.
USA CANADA ENGLAND

KID BUILDER BOOKS
Survival Kit for Families
Friendships Made to Last
Life Under Construction
Do-It-Yourself Bible Fun
Super Meetings for Kids
Incredible Meetings for Kids
Fantastic Meetings for Kids
Terrific Meetings for Kids

CONTRIBUTORS

Dale and Sandy Larsen have published books for kids and adults and are from Wisconsin.
Bernice Karnop is a teacher and writer from Great Falls, Montana.
Lin Johnson is a former college instructor and writes and leads workshops on working with young people.
Wendy Hunt, from Washington State, is a writer and educational therapist for the learning disabled.
Marion Duckworth is a seminar leader and the former president of the Oregon Association of Christian Writers; she has had several books published.
Loreli Dickerson is the former top editor of *Moody Magazine* and is now a children's books product manager in the Chicago area.

Scripture quotations, unless otherwise indicated, are from the *Holy Bible, New International Version*, © 1973, 1978, 1984, International Bible Society. Used by permission of Zondervan Bible Publishers.

ISBN: 0-89693-926-X

1 2 3 4 5 6 7 8 9 10 Printing/Year 95 94 93 92 91

CONTENTS

Introduction: Using *Super Meetings for Kids* 7
An introduction to what's included, how to use it, and the kids it's for.

Suggestions for Prayer and for Evangelism 10
Quick suggestions for helping a child find Christ and for prayer as a group.

1 Parents Are People Too: Knowing and Understanding Parents 11
Your kids will get a glimpse of what it's like to parent them, and will begin to understand what their parents do all day.

IDEAS FOR A MINISERIES ON DEALING WITH EMOTIONS 23
Using sessions 2–5 to help kids understand and handle their emotions—complete with ideas for an informal party.

2 Be Glad You're Not Mr. Spock: Understanding Your Emotions 27
God gave us our feelings and He'll help us manage them; help kids identify their feelings and get tips on ways to handle them.

3 Danger: Explosion Ahead: Dealing with Anger 35
Anger is a very powerful emotion, and this session will help your kids express it constructively.

4 Big Fear, Bigger God: Handling Fears 45
Help your kids learn how to handle situations even when they're petrified.

5 It's the Pits: Dealing with Sorrow and Disappointment 55
Help your kids recover from the pain we feel when we're disappointed in ourselves, others, or just life in general.

6 God's Plan for the Sexes: Christians and Homosexuality 63
Unfortunately, homosexuality has become an issue even for young kids. Help them see God's perspective on it and develop healthy friendships through this low-key lesson.

7 It's My Turn Now: Taking the Initiative to Change the Things I Can 71
Kids don't have to wait for adults to call the shots; encourage them in this session to take responsibility for growing and accomplishing on their own.

8 In Their Shoes: Helping a Friend by Showing Compassion 81
Sometimes a friend hurts terribly, sometimes a friend is experiencing hardship that looks like it will last for years. Help your kids be sensitive and show they care.

IDEAS FOR A MINISERIES ON THE CHURCH 89
Using sessions 9–11 to help your kids understand and appreciate God's people—complete with plans for an evening that includes a dramatic production and great food.

9 **How's This Monster Work? How the Church Works** 95
To kids, church often looks like an unfriendly monster made up of millions of other people's pet projects. Help them understand what the church is here for and how their particular church is organized.

10 **Coding the Facts into Pictures: Symbols in Our Church** 101
God has given us some pictures of deep truths; help your kids understand them through this lesson.

11 **The Next-Greatest Story Ever Told: The Church Through History** 107
Let your kids look at the wonderful stories of how God has worked in His people through centuries of breathtaking history.

12 **Body Builders: Physical Appearance** 121
How do I look? And how important is it how I look, anyway? Help your kids think of God's perspective and glean some practical tips for lookin' good.

An Evaluation from You: Did It Work? 127
Here's your chance to help design future Kid Builders products.

Super Meetings for Kids is a set of easy-to-use, relevant meeting plans for kids in grades 4 to 6, around the ages of 8 to 12. These plans are so easy to use, by the way, that it's not a necessity that you read this introduction. However, if you have time, it will make some things clearer and give you helpful tips you can use right away in your teaching.

These sessions are designed for maximum flexibility for the widest differences in individuals and groups. We assume that none of your current students have arrived in heaven yet, so they're well acquainted with problems; these sessions address a lot of common ones. In this book in the *Kid Builders* are sessions covering such problems as anger, knowing our parents, compassion for friends, homosexuality, physical appearance, the church, and emotions. (See the contents page for some more quick details.)

HOW TO USE *SUPER MEETINGS FOR KIDS*

When to Use These Plans

Sessions can be used in any order and in any situation you wish—"any old time." They require no more than 15 minutes of preparation time for the basic lesson—some optional activities take more time. You'll find the materials for the basic lesson in any average supply drawer—Bibles, pencils, pens, paper, glue, scissors. You'll also need access to a photocopier for making copies of the reproducible sheets.

When you're in a hurry, the most important sections to glance over before your meeting begins are the Goals list and Preparation list, both near the beginning of the lesson.

The basic lesson plan will take you about 45 minutes to cover; there are options galore for you to expand the session, and if you don't have enough time you can cut back on what you feel would be least helpful or interesting to your kids (that may be a hard choice!).

Here's a description of what each of the sections in a meeting plan includes, with ideas for their use.

Lesson Overview

At the beginning of each meeting plan is a lesson overview section just for leaders. It includes a catchy title that you can use in publicity, followed by a more definitive title to help you know what the session addresses. Next you'll see the Key Concept, which summarizes the fact you'll want your students to walk away with, and the main Scriptures on which the lesson is based; the Goals section elaborates on specific results you'll want to see from this lesson.

The Background section is for teachers who have time for more preparation. It's designed to help you get thinking about the lesson, along with ideas for places to get more information on the lesson's topic.

The Background section is followed by the Preparation list. This includes everything you'll need to do besides the obvious "Turn on the lights." The list includes any special materials you'd need for optional activities, but these are clearly marked as optional. Please note, though, that materials are not listed here for the expansion ideas at the end of the lessons, since they are usually more open-ended as well as more complicated.

Lesson Plan

One of the first things you'll notice about *Super Meetings for Kids* is the wide variety of teaching methods and types of lesson plans. That's part of the fun, and it's well organized so you'll never get lost. Each step is clearly numbered and takes you through a logical teaching order—from fun introductions to meatier lessons to practical conclusions. Each step is labeled with what type of activity it uses and what that activity teaches. Any suggestions for specific things to say are in **boldface.**

Many steps are followed by an "Alternative Approach." If you have time before your meeting, you'll want to see which approach you prefer—if you don't have time, you can just follow the regular lesson plan.

Interspersed among the regular activities are "Optional Activities." These are activities that bring in more information for your kids, or that offer fun activities that the basic plan may not have time for.

Most lesson plans will refer you to reproducible sheets, which you will find at the end of each appropriate lesson plan. The Preparation list will tell you how many copies you will need of each.

Lesson plans end with Ideas for Expanding This Lesson, a section of ideas that emphasize applying what the kids learned.

Additional Features

Super Meetings for Kids has plans for two miniseries that are appropriate for such events as summer camp or a series of church meetings for which you need to provide activities for the children. Each of the lessons within the suggested series stands fine alone; they work fine together as well.

Along with these two series ideas are plans for two parties. The first will help your kids understand their feelings, supplementing the four lessons on emotions. The second party is a chance to share with others what your kids learn in the three sessions on the church.

Parents are very important in your ministry, so *Friendships Made to Last* includes ideas for special activities that involve them.

For your convenience, there is a quick-reference page of ideas for helping a child meet Christ and for praying with kids, just after this introduction.

A FINAL NOTE ON THE LESSONS

We assume you know that *Super Meetings for Kids* is neither inspired nor inerrant. Please be creative and rearrange and adapt as you wish.

You and your kids are the reason for *Super Meetings for Kids.* Be sure to let us know what you think about it by filling out the evaluation form in the back.

A WORD ABOUT KIDS

The most important word to say about kids is that they're all different. Try to get to know your students individually; the most complete list of characteristics for 8–12-year-olds will never substitute for getting to know your own students.

If 8–12-year-olds are a new breed to you (come on, don't tell us you're under 8 yourself), it might help you to know that in preparing these sessions we had in mind kids who live in today's world . . . who love activity and noise . . . who want to learn if it's presented in an interesting way to them . . . to whom the group is often very important . . . who hate being embarrassed and who love fairness . . . who are at least beginning to ask the deepest questions of life . . . who need concrete examples of how to apply God's truths to all their lives. It's a great age group to get to know! Enjoy it!

HELPING A CHILD MEET CHRIST

Helping a child meet Christ can be one of the most joyful things to ever happen to you. Here are some suggestions:

A. Tell the child that the Gospel is the Good News that

(1) though we are sinners and deserve to die for our sin,

(2) God became a man—Jesus—and died for our sins; and

(3) we need to receive Jesus as our own Savior from sin, to "believe in the Lord Jesus Christ"—that Jesus died and rose from the dead—so that we can live forever with Him.

B. Don't push a child to receive Christ; the results of your telling the Gospel, as you know, are up to God Himself.

C. If a child does receive Christ, help him or her "grow"—talking to his newfound Savior, reading His Book, and enjoying His people are important parts of being a joyful Christian.

PRAYING WITH KIDS

Lots of kids feel uncomfortable praying in front of a group. You can help alleviate their discomfort by different approaches, such as those below. Also, as a general rule, don't single out a child to pray; ask for volunteers, but don't draft anyone.

Different approaches to group prayer:

Conversational prayer. Everybody closes their eyes and listens, but not everyone needs to pray. Whoever wishes to can say a sentence-or-two prayer out loud, then stop and give others a chance. A person can pray again later in the prayertime if he wishes.

Sentence prayers. Stand or sit in a circle and go around the circle, praying one-sentence prayers. If someone does not wish to pray, he just says "Amen" when it's his turn.

Card prayers. Have children write out short prayers on cards and have one child or leader read them aloud. The kids can keep their prayers anonymous if they wish.

Composed prayers. Have the whole group compose a prayer and read it out loud together prayerfully.

Parents Are People Too
or, Knowing and Understanding Parents

• KEY CONCEPT

Parents are real people with feelings and responsibilities.

• SCRIPTURES

Deuteronomy 6:4-7; Psalm 78:5-7; Proverbs 29:15, 17; Ephesians 6:4; Colossians 3:21

• GOALS

General: The students will understand that their parents have feelings like they do and are trying to fulfill their God-given responsibilities.
Specific: Students will be able to

A. describe ideal parents
B. discover their parents' feelings and responsibilities
C. thank their parents for specific actions

• BACKGROUND

This lesson: Relationships between children and parents are rarely ideal. Not all parents are as understanding as the Cosbys or as unobtrusive as those of the Degrassi High kids. Problems don't come packaged in 22-minute segments of introduction and resolution as in TV sitcoms. But even though the real world bears little resemblance to its media counterparts, most of your kids are not facing major conflicts with their parents. Most of the time, their biggest problems are taking their parents for granted and not understanding them.

Although one class period cannot entirely solve these problems, this lesson can help your students begin to grasp the fact that their parents are real people with the same kinds of feelings they have and that God has given them specific responsibilities to fulfill as they raise their children.

As you prepare this lesson, think about the families your students come from. Try to anticipate the kinds of responses they may give to such activities as naming problems they have with their parents (Step 2) and talking about how their parents are practicing God's commands (Step 3). As a result, you may want to omit an activity or substitute one that is less sensitive. Or spend more time helping your students think of positive characteristics and actions of their parents (Step 4).

For your further study: If you have extra time, consider these resources. The first two are written for teens but contain helpful information for teaching upper elementary kids too.

How to Live With Your Parents Without Losing Your Mind by Ken Davis (Zondervan, 1989).

Communication: Key to Your Parents by Rex Johnson (Harvest House, 1978).
Youth and Parents Together: Facing Life's Struggles, leaders' guide and participants' book by Mike Gillespie (Group Books, 1988). A 13-week curriculum course for junior highers and their parents that will give you additional ideas that can be adapted for juniors.
Ministry to Families with Teenagers by Dub Ambrose and Walt Mueller (Group Books, 1988). Includes a section of programming ideas that can be adapted for juniors, including a parent appreciation night.
Parents & Children edited by Jay Kesler, Ron Beers, and LaVonne Neff (Victor Books, 1986).

• PREPARATION

1. Gather one note card, pencil, Bible, and marking pen for each child.
2. Have masking tape available.
3. Make enough photocopies of reproducible sheet 1-A to string the figures around your classroom. Have at least two copies per child. Cut out the figures. (You can cut several sheets at one time.)
4. Make photocopies of reproducible sheet 1-B, enough for each kid.
5. Have a chalkboard or sheet of poster board available for writing.
6. Ask God to help your kids love and understand their parents more.
For alternative and optional activities (see below):
Gather two sheets of blank paper, one envelope, and one stamp for each child.
Make copies of reproducible sheet 1-C, one for each student.

STEP 1

MEDIA PARENTS
Circle Conversation

Ask: **If you could choose your own parents from those on TV, in a book, or in the movies, who would you choose and why?** Give students a minute to think; then go around the circle and have everyone respond.

Summarize by saying: **Even though we'd sometimes like to, we don't get to choose our parents. God has already made that choice for us. But there are some things we can do to get to know and understand our parents better so we can get along better.**

Alternative Approach
Ask students to describe the ideal parent.
Then use the summary above.

OPTIONAL ACTIVITY

Interviewing
Have some parents visit your classroom. *They should only be there for this activity,* so that all your kids will be open to sharing in the other activities. Interview the visiting parents as in a talk show, using reproducible sheet 1-C as a guide.

STEP 2

PROBLEMS WITH PARENTS
Discussion

Say: **Parents aren't perfect people. Sometimes we have problems with them—and sometimes they do with us.** Distribute note cards and pencils. Ask students to list some problems they have with their parents; don't have them add their names. Collect the cards and list the problems on the chalkboard or a sheet of poster board.

Starting with the top problem, ask group members to tell how they feel when they have that problem. Then ask them to tell how they think their parents feel. When you get to the end of the list, point out that parents are people too. They have feelings just like kids do, and get upset in situations like these. Most parents are doing their best to raise their children well, even though it's not easy. You may want to mention very briefly that some parents are abusive, though, and that kids should get help if that is happening.

Alternative Approach
Distribute blank sheets of paper and pencils. Instruct group members to each write a Dear Abby letter about a problem he has with his parents and sign it with a made-up name. When everyone is finished, collect the papers. One at a time, read each letter. Then ask group members to tell how they feel when they have that problem. Then ask them to tell how they think their parents feel. Continue with the instructions above.

STEP 3

PARENTS' RESPONSIBILITIES
Scripture Search

Say: **God has given parents specific responsibilities. Let's find out what some of them are.** One at a time, have group members read the following passages and name what God tells parents to do and any reasons God gives for that command. Then ask for specific ways their parents are obeying these instructions with them. Be sensitive to the fact that not even all "Christian" parents will be obeying these commands.

Deuteronomy 6:4-7—Love God, obey Him, and teach His commandments to their children throughout the day.

Psalm 78:5-7—Teach God's rules to their children so they will trust God and obey Him too.

Proverbs 29:15, 17—Discipline children for doing wrong.

Ephesians 6:4—Don't exasperate (nag, abuse authority, overly protect) children. Discipline and teach children God's Word.

Colossians 3:21—Don't embitter, or discourage, children.

Discuss: **Do you think it's easy for parents to obey all these commands God has given them? Why or why not? How can you help your parents obey God in raising you?**

STEP 4

PRAISING PARENTS
Listing

Say: **We've talked about problems we've had with our parents and looked at some of the responsibilities God has given them. Now let's**

think about what we like about our parents. Give everyone several paper figures from reproducible sheet 1-A and a marking pen. Have them write one thing on each figure that they like about their parents. After they each label some, have them tape the hands together to form a long string of figures. Starting in one corner, tape one end to a wall. Encourage everyone to list as many positive things about their parents as they can in order to string the figures around the entire room.

When the group is finished, have them walk around the room and read what they wrote. Point out common likes.

Alternative Approach

If you didn't have enough time to make and cut out *this* many figures, instead make enough to stretch across one whole wall. Kids can write more than one "like" on each figure.

OPTIONAL ACTIVITY

Cheer

Divide your students into groups of 4 or 5, appoint leaders, and give everyone a sheet of paper. Instruct them to write a cheer for their parents and prepare to present it to the rest of the class.

STEP 5

THANK YOU, GOD

Prayer

Say: **There are lots of things about our parents that we like. But too often we forget these and think only about the problems. Let's stop right now and thank God for our parents.** Have volunteers thank God for specific items listed on the paper figures.

STEP 6

DEAR PARENTS

Letters

Distribute copies of reproducible sheet 1-B and pencils. Have everyone write a letter to their parents, thanking them for specific actions and telling them they love them. Instruct students to give these letters to their parents.

Alternative Approach

Instead of having students deliver their letters, mail them. Give everyone a stamped envelope and pen. Have each person address the envelope to his parents and seal his letter inside. After class, mail the letters. Or if there is a mailbox nearby, have the class walk there together and deposit their letters.

OPTIONAL ACTIVITY

Get-Acquainted Questionnaire
Distribute copies of reproducible sheet 1-C. Challenge your group members to get to know their parents better by asking them the questions on the sheet. Emphasize that they must ask the questions and fill in the answers themselves; they are not to give the sheet to their parents and have them fill it out.

IDEAS FOR EXPANDING THIS LESSON

Plan a party or activity with your students and their parents or a parents' appreciation dinner. As part of the program, you may want to ask several parents to tell what it was like living with their parents when they were the same age as your students. Also have your students perform the cheers they wrote for their parents. (Be sure to collect at least one copy of each cheer.) For specific suggestions which can be adapted for juniors, see Ministry to Families with Teenagers *in the list of resources.*

Dear

Love,

Ask one or both of your parents the following questions, and record their answers.

1. What is your favorite food?

2. What is your favorite color?

3. What is your favorite sport?

4. What is your favorite animal?

5. What is your favorite holiday? Why?

6. What did you like to do most when you were my age?

7. What was your favorite subject in school? What did you like about it?

8. When you were my age, what did you want to be when you grew up?

9. What is your favorite thing about your job?

10. What is your least favorite thing about your job?

11. If you could vacation anywhere in the world, where would you go? Why?

12. If you had a day to yourself and money was no object, what would you do?

Getting to Know Me
or, Ideas for a Party
Using Lessons 2–5 on Emotions

Plan an informal party in a location where kids can relax: your home perhaps, or out-of-doors.

Tell them that they're going to have a chance to get acquainted with the person they need to know best: themselves. Hand out reproducible sheet "All About Me" and pencils, to be filled out in the below order. After each activity, have a discussion time about what they wrote on their sheets. Help them see how these things can help them have healthy emotions.

Activity 1, MUSIC: Play a variety of kinds of music: marches, soft instrumentals, upbeat pieces, etc. Have them write how each makes them feel and fill out the rest of that section.

Activity 2, COLORS: Pass around various colors of construction paper and have them fill out the chart on the sheet.

Activity 3, GAMES: Set up various board games and give about 15 minutes to play. Use this to explore afterward their feelings about winning and losing.

Activity 4, WORDS: Play this game: Form a circle. Say, **You have five seconds to call out a word that completes the sentence or you're out of the circle.** After a minute or so, reverse the direction and give another sentence for them to complete. Reward those left in the circle.

A word that makes me feel happy is . . .
A word that makes me feel sad is . . .
A word that makes me feel angry is . . .
A word that makes me feel excited is . . .
A word that makes me feel disgusted is . . .
A word that makes me feel peaceful is . . .

Have them fill out the "WORDS" section of their sheet after the game.

In addition, you may want to review the previous sessions on emotions, anger, etc., and do activities you didn't have time for during class. Have kids enter results under: "More Things I'm Learning About Myself."

At the end, serve refreshments that make kids feel good, and sing songs that do too. Encourage them to keep filling out their sheets at home as they learn more about their emotions.

Things I'm Learning About Me

MUSIC

KIND | HOW IT MAKES ME FEEL

Music to listen to when I'm sad:

when I'm angry:

when I'm afraid:

COLORS

NAME | HOW IT MAKES ME FEEL

Colors I wear or have in my room are important because . . .

Colors that cheer me up:

Colors that make me feel peaceful:

GAMES

Winning games makes me feel . . .

Losing makes me feel . . .

How upset do I get when I lose?

What I need to keep in mind when I play is . . .

WORDS

THAT MAKE ME FEEL

sad:

angry:

excited:

disgusted:

peaceful:

What kind of words can I use to make others feel good?

MORE THINGS I'M LEARNING ABOUT MYSELF

Be Glad You're Not Mr. Spock or, Understanding Your Emotions

part 1 of miniseries
Dealing with Emotions

• KEY CONCEPT

God created us with the ability to experience emotions, and rightly used they are one of His best gifts.

• SCRIPTURES

Genesis 1:27; 3:10; Psalm 6:6; 54:4; 1 John 4:16

• GOALS

General: Kids will see that experiencing all kinds of emotions is a part of being a human created by God, and that He'll help them manage their feelings.
Specific: Learners will be able to

A. identify different feelings, both pleasant and painful
B. realize that feelings are temporary and changing
C. understand that the ability to have emotions is the way all of us are created
D. realize that both pleasant and unpleasant emotions are necessary to be a human being
E. discover ways to handle their feelings

• BACKGROUND

This lesson: Kids 8 to 12 are becoming very aware of their feelings. Some of their emotions can be overwhelming. Now is the time for them to think about the kinds of feelings they have, and to realize that it's normal to have them.

But kids are also being sold the idea that feeling good is all that counts and the world around them provides a lot of ways to make that happen. That's why it's important to get a biblical perspective on where their emotions came from and the purposes that God intends them to serve.

For your further study: If you have extra time, consider these:
Emotions: Can You Trust Them? by James Dobson (Bantam, 1982)
The Christian's Use of Emotional Power by H. Norman Wright (Fleming H. Revell, 1974)

• PREPARATION

1. Have a stack of 30 or so index, cards or papers about that size.
2. Have a pencil for each student.
3. Have a chalkboard and chalk, or a substitute, available.
4. Make photocopies of reproducible sheets 2-A and 2-B for each student.
5. Pray that God will help your kids understand about emotions.

For alternative and optional activities (see below):
Gather a piece of paper and at least five crayons for each student.

STEP 1

DISCOVERING THE DIFFERENT WAYS WE FEEL
Writing About Emotions

Hand out pencils and copies of reproducible sheet 2-A. Have students fill out "How I'd Feel" for each of the situations.

Have volunteers read their answers to each situation, one at a time. List their words on the chalkboard. Have a student copy one word each on a stack of cards.

Ask the children to define the word *emotion* if they can. Write on the chalkboard definitions such as "a strong feeling; any reaction to a situation."

Then brainstorm and list other emotions (e.g., hopefulness, eagerness, disgust). Have the student continue to make the word cards.

Alternative Approach
Write your definition of emotions on the board. Give a couple of examples, (e.g., fear, eagerness), then provide pencil and a stack of cards, and give the group three minutes to come up with a list of as many different feelings as they can think of. Talk about times when they have experienced one of these emotions.

If there are any duplicate cards, discard them before Step 2.

OPTIONAL ACTIVITY

Sharing
If you have time, let your students share some "emotional times."

When have you had an experience similar to the ones we listed?

You may then want to share a time you experienced a strong emotion, and what happened as a result.

STEP 2

CATEGORIZING FEELINGS
A Demonstration

Distribute one card from Step 1 to each student and have your kids line up in front of the room. (If your group is small, lay cards on a table.) Ask another student to separate them into two groups: pleasant emotions and unpleasant emotions. Have others decide whether they agree or disagree, and make necessary changes.

Say: **Very likely we experience several of these emotions in a given day.** Ask a student to come up and choose ones they might feel in a day.

Point out that it's normal for our emotions to change. We may be angry, happy, disgusted, and sad in only a few hours.

STEP 3

BE GLAD YOU'RE NOT MR. SPOCK
A Skit

Suppose a space ship landed from another planet. Like those from which Mr. Spock's father came, these people have no emotions. (If necessary, have a student explain who Spock is—a character on "Star Trek," the TV show and films.) **The outer-space people see you laugh and cry and become angry, and they want you to explain why it is that you act that way.**

Hand out and assign the roles from reproducible sheet 2-B (three extraterrestrials, four earthlings; you can "double up" if necessary). Let each performer look over his part. Have extraterrestrials and earthlings sit opposite each other and the rest of the group sit down as the audience. Perform the skit. (You'll discuss it later.)

STEP 4

HAPPY ALL THE TIME? NO WAY!
Robots

Select a few students to stand in front and play the part of robots. Explain that they've been programmed to be happy all the time. They can experience no other emotion.

Select a few students to stand in front and be themselves—ordinary human beings. Read each of the situations on reproducible sheet 2-A and let the "robots" pantomime their happy response; then give the "normal human beings" a chance to pantomime the normal response.

When you're finished, ask, **What's wrong with being happy all the time?** Point out that the ability to be sad when your dog dies shows that he was important to you. Ask: **Would you want to laugh when you got that kind of news? When a friend tells you that her parents are getting a divorce? Why not?**

OPTIONAL ACTIVITY

Art
Provide crayons and paper and let kids make a design in which colors of their choice represent the following emotions: anger, love, sadness, peacefulness, and excitement. Talk about color choices they made.

STEP 5

HANDLING UNPLEASANT EMOTIONS
A Story and Discussion

Our feelings are our reactions to things that happen to us. David defeated the giant, Goliath, with a slingshot, and that made him feel pretty happy. When Moses received the Ten Commandments on the top of Mount Sinai, he must have felt pretty amazed and overwhelmed.

Unpleasant feelings are hardest to handle. Sometimes they are pretty strong and can last a long time.

(Read the following story aloud.) **They did for Bill. His best friend moved away and Bill was miserable.**

"I'll never have a friend as good as Dick," he thought.

Every day after school, Bill came home and just sat in his room instead of practicing swimming with the team or shooting baskets with

his brother. His dad came to his room and tried to talk to him, but Bill just mumbled and scratched the dog. He stopped praying before he went to bed because he just didn't feel like it.

Kids called and asked him to go bike riding, but Bill sighed over the phone as though he just didn't have any energy and said, "Uh-uhh" and hung up.

Pretty soon, they stopped calling. His brother shot baskets with someone else; the coach said if Bill didn't practice he'd be off the team.

"I don't care," Bill told himself. "They just don't understand how terrible I feel because Dick is gone."

Ask: **What's wrong with the way Bill acted after Dick left?** Ideas: It's normal to be sad when a friend leaves, but if that's all we think about, it can turn into self-pity. Then we don't realize God has given us other friends and fun things to do.)

What things that he stopped doing would help Bill? (Keep swimming, be friends with his brother, go bike riding with the kids, tell God how he feels. He could write Dick a letter too.)

Close by reminding students that emotions are a gift from God, but they're only part of us. It's important to say how we feel and to get help from a mature adult when a particular feeling becomes overpowering.

Thank God together that He created us with the ability to have feelings.

IDEAS FOR EXPANDING THIS LESSON

Provide an opportunity for kids to experience one of the most positive feelings they can have—the satisfaction of helping someone. It could be yard work for a shut-in or for the church. Afterward, plan a refreshment time and informal discussion of how doing the work made them feel. You may want Helping Day to be a regular event.

Also see the party plan at the beginning of this series for ideas on expanding your meetings on emotions.

HOW WOULD YOU FEEL?

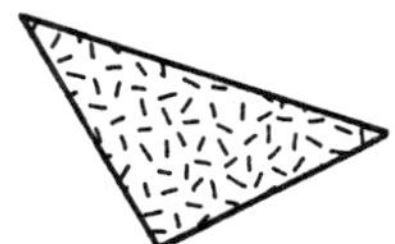

Situation	How I'd Feel—in One Word
Someone steals your bike	
A tiny baby holds your finger	
Your team wins the championship	
Your mom discovers the report card you hid	
Your dog dies	
You stand up to give a talk to the class and forget everything you're supposed to say	
You climb a mountain and finally get to the top where you look at the scenery below	
Another kid gets the band solo even though you are a much better player	

W·E·L·C·O·M·E T·O EMOTIONAL E·A·R·T·H

EARTHLING 1: We welcome you to Planet Earth. What questions would you like to ask us?

EXTRATERRESTRIAL 1: We notice that you have things you call "emotions." Where did they come from?

EARTHLING 2: God created us like Himself, and the Bible says that He has emotions. "God created man in His own image, in the image of God He created him," it says in God's Book (Genesis 1:27).

EXTRATERRESTRIAL 2: Are you the only people who have emotions, or do all humans have them?

EARTHLING 3: All humans from the beginning of time have had feelings like us. The first man, Adam, said, "I was afraid . . . so I hid" (Genesis 3:10).

EARTHLING 4: Our King David felt sad. He said, "I'm worn out from groaning. All night long I flood my bed with weeping" (Psalm 6:6). He also felt hopeful: "Surely God is my help" (Psalm 54:4).

EXTRATERRESTRIAL 3: What good are emotions?

EARTHLING 1: They enable us to be like God in certain ways. For example, the Bible says, "God is love" (1 John 4:16). That means He not only thinks lovingly about us but feels lovingly toward us too. We humans can feel close to one another because we have the ability to feel love for one another.

EXTRATERRESTRIAL 1: But can't emotions cause problems?

EARTHLING 2: Yes. Humans are sinful, and so we can hate people and hurt them when we're emotional.

EXTRATERRESTRIAL 3: What can you do about that?

EARTHLING 3: God can help us use our emotions the way He wants.

DANGER: Explosion Ahead or, Dealing with Anger

part 2 of miniseries
Dealing with Emotions

• KEY CONCEPT

Anger is a normal, powerful emotion that we can learn to express constructively.

• SCRIPTURES

Exodus 4:14; Numbers 12:9: Matthew 21:12-13; Proverbs 16:32; Ephesians 4:26; James 1:19-20

• GOALS

General: The student will see that he or she has the ability to express his or her anger without getting in trouble; in fact some good can come out of it.
Specific: Students will be able to

A. understand what makes them angry and how anger feels
B. explore ways they respond when angry
C. explain that being angry isn't sinful
D. understand that they can decide whether to react constructively or destructively

• BACKGROUND

This lesson: All kids become angry, but some show it more than others. The ones who explode and the ones who internalize both need to learn what to do with that powerful emotion.

Kids have reasons to become angry these days. Parents divorce, families move frequently, home life is unstable; and these things may seem unfair. Since they're powerless to do anything to change situations like these, their anger can create ongoing problems unless they learn how to deal with it.

They also have to handle the everyday "I'm mad at you" tiffs kids have. Now is the time for them to acquire basic information and skills for both kinds of situations. This lesson will help equip them.

For your further study:
Anger: Yours and Mine and What to Do About It! by Richard P. Walters (Zondervan, 1981)

• PREPARATION

1. Have chalkboard and chalk available.
2. Make copies of sheets 3-A and 3-B for each student.
3. Have a pencil for every student.
4. Pray that God will help your students control their anger.
For alternative and optional activities (see below):
Get treats for the game in Step 2.

STEP 1

WHAT MAKES YOU ANGRY?
Activity Sheet

Instruct students to fill out reproducible sheet 3-A. After they're finished, ask what situations made them most angry and least angry and why.

Ask them to call out words or phrases that describe how they feel when "in real life" they "hit the top" of the Mad-o-meter (*steamed, hot, boiling mad, ready to explode*). Point out that those expressions denote strong feelings and that, when we become very angry, that emotion takes over and that's about all we can think about.

STEP 2

WAYS WE REACT WHEN WE'RE ANGRY
Draw-and-Guess Game

Divide students into two teams and have individuals from each team alternate in drawing pictures on the chalkboard of a way they might react when they are very angry. Allow one minute for their teammates to guess what it depicts. Award one point for each second it takes for them to guess the answer—60 points if they fail to guess correctly. A team retires if they fail to identify two drawings. The team with the *least* points wins.

When you finish playing, ask, **Do you decide to act in a certain way when you get angry, or does it just happen?** (Usually, it just happens.) **Do some of the ways we respond when we're angry get us in trouble? Which ones? How does that make things worse?** (We're still angry, only now we're in trouble too.)

Alternative Approach
Have small treats for the winning team.

STEP 3

SEEING ANGER THE WAY GOD DOES
Bible Activity

Write the following question on the chalkboard: "Is it sinful to be angry?"

Have volunteers read aloud Exodus 4:14 and Numbers 12:9. Ask, **Who is the person who's angry in those passages?** (God) **We know that anger isn't sinful because God becomes angry, and He isn't sinful. So what's the answer to our question on the board? Do you think there's a difference between God's anger and ours? We'll find the answer later on.**

Have students read reproducible sheet 3-B and fill in answers only to situations 1–4. When they're finished, make sure all their answers are "poor." Ask, **What made each of these people angry? Was it a good reason or a poor reason?** (Poor: Cain was jealous; Naaman was impatient; the Jews were prejudiced and ignorant; the Ephesians were ignorant and greedy.) Discuss also their violent responses to their anger and the people to whom it caused pain.

Ask students to do Situation 5 on the sheet. Talk about the fact that Jesus had good reasons to become angry because God's house was being used wrongly. His response was to change that. Explain that God's anger grows out of unselfish reasons, not selfish ones. Review the fact that to feel angry isn't wrong. We need to decide if we're angry for the wrong reasons, though, and make sure it is not hurting ourselves and others.

Alternative Approach
If not all in your group read well or work well independently, have them work in small groups with older students assigned to read Situations 1–4 aloud. Have them decide answers together.

STEP 4

CONTROLLING ANGER
Listing

Read each of the following passages. Then, after each, have students tell what they learned about controlling their reactions to things that make them angry. Make a list of their ideas on the chalkboard during the discussion.
Proverbs 16:32 (Learn to be patient and control your temper.)
Ephesians 4:26 (Choose good ways to express your anger. Get rid of your angry feelings the same day.)
James 1:19-20 (Learn to be quick to listen to the other person's side, and slow to say nasty things because too often the way we express our anger causes pain to ourselves and others.)

STEP 5

HOW ONE GIRL LEARNED TO HANDLE HER ANGER
A True Story

Read the following story aloud. **I'm Helen. I was 14 when I lost control of my bike and was hit by a truck. Doctors told me I'd never walk again. The worst hurt came when my mother told me in the hospital, "You can't come home." She didn't have time to take care of a handicapped daughter.**

"How can God do this to me?" I raged. After that, I lived in seven foster homes. I'd test the people's love by acting obnoxiously. I cursed and threw things and once even put my fist through a wall.

Then someone told me that God loved me, and I renewed the relationship with Jesus I'd begun as a child. A counselor helped me realize I was angry with my parents for rejecting me. Every day as I drove to college, I memorized Scripture and asked God to change the way I thought. I put up notes to myself to think "God thoughts" instead of angry ones. I forgave my mom too.

People began noticing the change in me. They said I was more fun to be with. I'm not angry anymore.

Use the following as discussion guides:

How would you feel if you had Helen's experience in the hospital?

What ways did she express her feelings? Whom did they harm? How?

What ways did she learn to control her anger?

What other ideas can we add? (Ideas: Take deep breaths, count to 10 a few times, take a walk, play basketball or some other active sport, talk to someone or to God.)

Which ideas could Cain, Naaman, the Jews, and the Ephesians have used?

Now think, which idea would you pick to respond to the situation on the "Mad-o-meter" that made you most angry? Have children think of their answer silently. **Is it the way you usually respond? If not, why not? What can you do differently?**

STEP 6

USE YOUR ANGER
Role Play

Remind kids that Jesus' anger was justified and He used it to do something worthwhile—to show that God's house was to be used for worship.

How could you use your anger in the following situations to accomplish something good?

You see some older kids picking on a little one. (Give time for your kids' ideas after each situation.)

You hear kids saying bad, untrue things about your friend.

A kid with a foreign accent enrolls in your school and others laugh at her and say she talks funny.

Your little brother thinks you're wonderful and wants to follow you wherever you go.

Close with prayer that God will show you all ways to use your anger to accomplish something good.

OPTIONAL ACTIVITY

Activity Story

Read through the following story and lead a discussion afterward. Ideas for discussion are listed at the end.

RED HOT TEMPER
A true story by Mark Winkelman
as told to Marion Duckworth

Losing my cool had become a way of life for me. I started battling with my fists when I was a kid. My father, a pastor, was transferred a lot, and that meant a new school every year. And every time, I had to face the problem of making friends.

There were always those who wanted to be anything *but* friends. The fact that I'd accepted Christ as my Savior when I was a little kid should have made a difference in my life. But I was more interested in winning Bible drills than applying Scripture where I needed it most—to my trigger temper.

One place I *really* had trouble was on the football field. I'd get mad if things didn't go right and take it out on the guy across from me by playing a little dirty ball, making sure the referee didn't see me.

I knew that without God's help, controlling my temper was pretty hopeless. When I finally started paying attention in Bible class, the Holy Spirit began showing me that God's Word wasn't just something to use for memory-verse contests.

One unit was on biblical principles that apply to a Christian athlete. "Find something that resembles a cross. Let it remind you of Jesus, as though He's there in person watching the game."

I chose the football goal post. The result amazed me. My angry feelings just passed over. I didn't want to wipe out my opponent. I

felt great. I knew then that I didn't have to lose my cool—if I kept my mind on Jesus.

I still feel angry sometimes (that's part of being human). But Jesus, not revenge, is the answer. I trust in God and ask Him to strengthen—not destroy—my relationships with other people.

Use the following ideas for discussion starters:

1. What other ways do kids show their anger besides fighting?

2. How could Mark have licked his temper earlier?

3. Why didn't knowing Jesus as Savior keep Mark from getting angry and fighting?

4. What other ways are there that you can take out your anger on others? (pick on younger brothers and sisters, talk back to adults)

5. How else can you find ways to remember that Jesus is present in all you do?

6. What's the difference between using Bible verses to win drills and to help you control your anger?

Encourage kids to talk about times when anger has affected their behavior and ways they can apply the principles Mark learned.

(Article about Mark Windleman based on one originally published in FREEWAY, Scripture Press.)

IDEAS FOR EXPANDING THIS LESSON

See the activity at the beginning of this series on Handling Emotions.

What Makes You Angry?

Mad-o-meter

Read the following situations and write down the number for each one on the Mad-o-meter where your response would be.

1. You have to take medicine that makes you gain weight, and kids in school make fun of you.
2. You have to wear a sweater your grandma made for you, and the kids think it is ugly and call you "dorky."
3. You just finish sorting a pile of school papers and someone turns on an electric fan and blows them all over the room.
4. Your mom promises to buy you art supplies but then has to use the money to get shoes for your baby brother.
5. You're next in line and a big kid pushes his way in front of you.

As angry as I can get. ○

Makes me want to slam doors ○

Angry enough to call names ○

Pretty stirred up ○

Mildly Irritated ○

You make me so MAD that I...

Read situations 1–4 and decide whether the people had a good or a poor reason for becoming angry, and whether they responded well to their anger or not. (Wait for instructions for situation 5.)

Situation 1: Cain became angry with his brother Abel because God accepted Abel's offering and not Cain's. So Cain killed his brother Abel. (Genesis 4:2-16)

☐ **Good Reason** ☐ **Good Response**

☐ **Poor Reason** ☐ **Poor Response**

Situation 2: Captain Naaman became angry because he wasn't cured of leprosy right away. Instead, God wanted him to dip seven times in the Jordan River and have faith that then he'd be healed. It was only because Naaman's servants talked him into it that he obeyed and was healed. (2 Kings 5:1-14)

☐ **Good Reason** ☐ **Good Response**

☐ **Poor Reason** ☐ **Poor Response**

Situation 3: The Jewish people were furious with Jesus because He claimed to be the Savior and said everyone, not only Jews, could be saved from sin. The Jewish people tried to kill Him. (Luke 4:16-30)

☐ **Good Reason** ☐ **Good Response**

☐ **Poor Reason** ☐ **Poor Response**

Situation 4: People who lived in the city of Ephesus were angry because the Apostle Paul spoke against their idols, and making idols was their business. A mob screamed at Paul. (Acts 19:23-41)

☐ **Good Reason** ☐ **Good Response**

☐ **Poor Reason** ☐ **Poor Response**

Situation 5: Jesus entered the temple and discovered it had turned into a mini shopping center. He accused them of making it into a den of robbers instead of a place of worship, and He overturned the tables of merchandise. (Matthew 21:12-13)

☐ **Good Reason** ☐ **Good Response**

☐ **Poor Reason** ☐ **Poor Response**

Big Fear, Bigger God or, Handling Fears

part 3 of miniseries Dealing with Emotions

• KEY CONCEPT

God is always ready to help us get over our fears.

• SCRIPTURES

John 18:25-27; Acts 18:6-10; Psalms 3:5-6; 56:3-4; Isaiah 41:10; 43:2; Matthew 6:25-27

• GOALS

General: Students will begin to face and overcome their fears.
Specific: Learners will be able to
A. explain that everyone has fear at some time or another
B. understand that we can get over a fear when we let God help us do so

• BACKGROUND

This lesson: Often children are taught that it's a sign of weakness to have fear. An adult may mean well when he or she says, "Don't be such a scaredy-cat. You're too big to be afraid." But statements like those only encourage a child to deny his fears. As a result, they fail to face and conquer them.

How much better to help them admit each fear, define it, and learn how to deal with it through the power of God. What a valuable skill to learn early in life! For that to happen, kids need to talk about different kinds of fears people have and the ones they've experienced themselves.

God makes many promises in Scripture to help us deal with our fears. With His help, children can admit a fear, and gradually learn to overcome it. It's important to keep in mind that some boys and girls are more impressionable than others and, as a result, are more prone to develop particular fears. Some fears may be severe and deep-seated and require additional help to become free of.

Kids need adults like you to be sensitive to them in this area and talk with them. Hopefully, your session on fear will provide an opportunity.

For your further study: If you have extra time, consider *Christian Counseling*, by Gary R. Collins (Word, 1980); chapter on "Anxiety."

• PREPARATION

1. Pray that God will help your children conquer their fears.
2. Gather one pencil and piece of paper for each child.
3. Make a copy of reproducible sheets 4-A and 4-B for each child.
4. Have about seven Bibles available.

For alternative and optional activities (see below):
Bring small treats.

Gather two more pieces of paper for each student.
Have a chalkboard available.

STEP 1

ME, AFRAID? YOU BET!
A Bragging Game

Have students stand in a circle. Each one gets five seconds to finish the sentence, "I'm so brave that I could . . . " The claims they make must be outlandish and daring ("go alone into a cage of lions"; "go swimming in the ocean when there's snow on the ground").

If someone can't make a wild statement in five seconds, he must sit down. Set a time limit, and if you wish, award small treats to those left standing when time is up.

Say, **It's unlikely that we'd really do the things we bragged we would. To be afraid of some things, like a dog who's bitten several people so we'll leave him alone, is smart. We may be able to stand here and pretend not to be afraid of anything, but in real life, that's not the way we are.**

Alternative Approach

This is a quieter opening activity. Give each student pencil and paper and read the following fears. As you do so, ask students to rate themselves as follows:
1. Not scared; 2. Scared; 3. Terrified

1. You're shut in a room full of spiders.
2. You have to pick up a snake.
3. You're alone in a deserted part of town late at night.
4. You have to wrestle a bully who's 6′6″ and has huge muscles.
5. You are standing on an outside ledge of a skyscraper.
6. Superman is holding your hand, ready to take you flying through space.
7. You're going on a spaceship to the moon.
8. You're going to dinner with the President of the United States.

Say, **We're all afraid of something if we're truthful with ourselves about it. There are times when we should be afraid, because that keeps us from getting hurt.** Use the example of a dog who's bitten several people.

STEP 2

DISCOVERING WHAT I'M AFRAID OF
Guessing Game

Have students complete reproducible sheet 4-A. Then give the answers (1 high places; 2 the dark; 3 of strong light; 4 of animals; 5 of being in closed places; 6 of open or public places; 7 of England; 8 of water; 9 of the number 13). Ask which fears they think are ones not many people have and which ones are quite common. **What other fears do people have that aren't on the list?** (Examples: being home alone, making a fool of yourself, that a parent will be mad at you, that you'll get hurt, that you'll do badly in school)

Alternative Approach

Write on the chalkboard the following list of what some say are the 13 worst human fears:

1. Speaking before a group

2. Heights
3. Insects and bugs
4. Financial problems
5. Deep water
6. Sickness
7. Death
8. Flying
9. Loneliness
10. Dogs
11. Driving/riding in a car
12. Elevators
13. Escalators

(from *The Book of Lists* by David Wallechinsky, Irving Wallace, and Amy Wallace; Bantam, 1978, p. 469)

Explain that more people are afraid of number 1; fewer of number 2; etc. Give each kid pencil and paper and time to choose the five things listed that they're most afraid of.

When everyone is done, have them compare their lists with one other person in the room. Have them tell the other person, if they want, what else they would put on the list.

STEP 3

MAN, WAS I SCARED
Drawing

Ask students to draw a picture of an experience they had when they were afraid and write a description of it on the back. *Tell them not to write their names on the paper.* Collect and have the group try to identify the types of fear from the drawings (e.g., a fear of getting hurt).

STEP 4

FAMOUS PEOPLE ARE AFRAID TOO
Radio Call-ins

Imagine you've been invited to be on a radio call-in program to talk about overcoming fear. The verses will help you answer questions from listeners like "Were people in the Bible ever afraid?" and "What scared people in Bible days?"

Assign students to read the following Scriptures aloud so kids can answer the two above questions. Be prepared to help by giving the information in parentheses if necessary.

John 18:25-27 (Peter was afraid of being known as a Christian because Jesus had been arrested and he thought that if they knew, they'd arrest him as well.)

Acts 18:6-10 (Paul was afraid of getting hurt for telling people about Jesus.) Have kids say out loud what they'd tell callers.

You'll also want to be able to tell the callers that the God who created them has promised to help them with their fears. Ask different students to read the below verses and have volunteers pretend to answer the phone and say what they'd tell callers. Proverbs 3:5-6; Psalm 56:3-4; Isaiah 41:10; 43:2; Matthew 6:25-27.

STEP 5

TAKE MY HAND
Faith Walk

Have students pair up and take one another on a faith walk around the room. The first student closes his eyes tightly, the second takes his hand and leads him. If time permits, allow the pairs to change roles. Explain that the purpose is to experience faith. You have to trust the other person not to walk you into a wall.

When done, ask them to describe their feelings. Explain, **We need to trust God to help us with a fear the way we had to trust our partner on a faith walk. We can't see God but He's there.**

What we need to remember is who God is. Have group call out words to describe God (all powerful; loving; our Friend). **If we remember who God is, we'll trust Him to help us even when we feel afraid. Sometimes we have to do something scary, but we can't let our feelings stop us. We have to go ahead and face it, even though we feel afraid, trusting God to see us through.**

Alternative Approach
If the whole group can't participate in a faith walk, have two volunteers do so, switching roles while the others watch. Have them describe their feelings, then follow with the discussion outlined above.

STEP 6

GETTING FREE OF A FEAR
Activity Sheet

Distribute reproducible sheet 4-B and have the group fill it in together. Read the advice given below, then let kids talk over what word or phrase to use to name the step of each rung and fill it in. They can write in additional notes if they wish.

Rung 1: **We need to tell God exactly what we're afraid of.** (Idea for summarizing word: PRAY.)

Rung 2: **We must decide if we want to get over our fear and are willing to do what's necessary. The kid in the drawing has a ladder provided to get out of the pit, but he has to climb out himself.** (DECIDE.)

Rung 3: **We need to face our fear every time it happens. Tell God how we feel and pray for His strength. Trust Him to provide it.** (Use experiences from this session as illustrations if you wish.) (FACE IT.)

Rung 4: **Always go slowly. Don't expect to get over a fear in one day. It takes time. Feelings of fear may remain for a while, but don't give up.** (PERSEVERE, OR KEEP GOING.)

Rung 5: **It's important to tell an understanding adult. Ask them to help you.** ("HELP!")

Rung 6: **Don't worry if the fear returns when you think you've licked it. Remember God's promise to help, and count on Him even though you don't feel like it.** (TRUST.)

OPTIONAL ACTIVITY

Write Psalm 56:3 on the chalkboard. Give kids a couple of minutes to decide which word in the verse they think is most important and why. Have them read the verse as a private prayer, then close by reading it aloud as a group prayer.

IDEAS FOR EXPANDING THIS LESSON

Plan an activity that most kids are afraid of, like speaking in front of a group. You could arrange for each to do so in your class or in a youth-oriented church service.

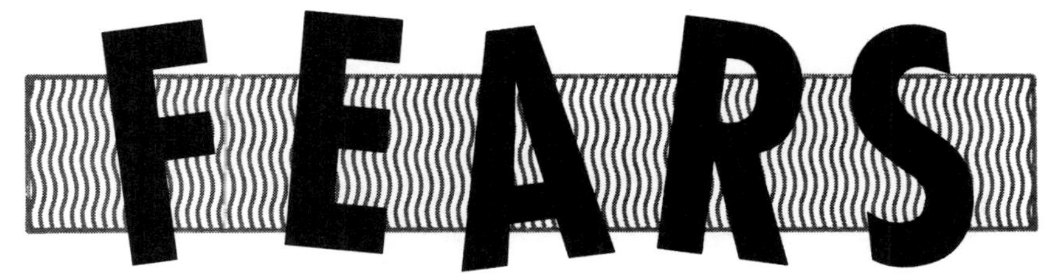

Draw a line from the name of the fear in column one to the definition in the second column. Since you probably have never heard of most of these, see how good you are at guessing the answers.

1. Acrophobia
2. Nyctophobia
3. Photophobia
4. Zoophobia
5. Claustrophobia
6. Agoraphobia
7. Anglophobia
8. Hydrophobia
9. Triskaidekaphobia

- Fear of animals
- Fear of high places
- Fear of water
- Fear of strong light
- Fear of open or public places
- Fear of being in closed places
- Fear of the dark
- Fear of England
- Fear of the number 13

HOW
TO GET
OVER
MY
FEAR

It's the Pits
or, Dealing with Sorrow and Disappointment

part 4 of miniseries
Dealing with Emotions

• KEY CONCEPT

Sadness and disappointment are painful, but God can help us recover.

• SCRIPTURES

1 John 1:9; John 1:10; Matthew 27:27-31; John 7:3-5; Matthew 11:28

• GOALS

General: Kids will explore the emotion of sadness and learn how to deal with it.
Specific: Students will be able to
A. explain that everyone feels sad sometimes
B. understand that feeling sad affects the way we act
C. understand that we share the same kinds of disappointment-making experiences
D. understand that guilt can make us dissappointed in ourselves
E. recognize that Jesus felt sorrowful and disappointed, so He understands
F. explain that going to Jesus for help is the first step to take when we are in the pits

• BACKGROUND

This lesson: Kids can't always put into words how they feel when something makes them sad or dissappointed. More likely, they'll act it out by retreating to their room, whining, or even becoming rebellious. That's why they need help in verbalizing what makes them sad, what their specific feelings are, and the problems they have in dealing with sorrow.

What makes kids sad? The same categories as adults, usually. The loss of someone or something important; their own failure or that of someone close to them; inability to achieve something important to them; being let down by a loved one. Another important reason kids feel down is guilt. They need to learn how to deal with the feelings and the problems that cause those feelings so that serious depression won't set in.

For your further study:
Coping with Teenage Depression by Kathleen McCoy (New American Library, 1982). Although written for a slightly older age group, it's still very helpful.

• PREPARATION

1. Pray that God will help your kids find His joy and believe in His mercy.
2. Make 4 copies of sheet 5-A and a copy for each child of 6-B.
3. Gather tape, enough sheets of newsprint or other paper for every child,

crayons or marking pens, and plain paper and pencils for each child.
4. Have a chalkboard.

STEP 1

WHAT'S YOUR PROBLEM?
A Skit

Distribute reproducible sheet 5-A to cast members: two boys and two girls. Give them time to read through the skit while you're singing or having other preliminaries. Set up three chairs at the front. Have the skit. After applause at the end, ask what was wrong with the way the kids related to one another. (Everyone thought his problems were the worst and wouldn't listen to anyone else's.) Point out that **everyone is in the pits sometimes. That's part of life. We can learn how to keep from staying there, though.**

STEP 2

BE A CLOWN
Designing

Provide sheets of paper or put up newsprint on the walls. Make sure there are enough crayons or marking pens for each student. Say that clowns are among the few people in the world who get paid to look sad. Each clown makeup is unique and specially designed to look the way the clown is supposed to feel.

Tell them they're going to design an original sad clown face. Encourage them to make it as unique as possible. **To put you in the mood, think of one thing that happened to you that made you feel sad or disappointed. Then draw your clown face.**

After they're done and have shared their drawings with the group, ask kids to show the kind of act their clowns would put on to show how sad they are. (For example, walk around looking at the ground; crying.) Say, **These are some of the ways we show that we're miserable.** Have volunteers tell the experience they thought of before they drew their clown faces, and write them on the chalkboard. (Do not erase.) How did they show their sadness at the time?

STEP 3

I'M SO ASHAMED
Finishing Stories

Sometimes the reason we feel sad is because we did something wrong. We feel guilty—disappointed in ourselves. Unless we do something about our guilt, it doesn't go away, does it?

The first question we have to ask ourselves is: "Why do I feel guilty? What specific thing did I do wrong?" Sometimes, we feel guilty but didn't do anything wrong.

Ask students to decide if the following kids did something wrong, and if so, what it was.

1. **Sam told his dad that his teacher didn't give the big test, because Sam had failed it.** (Yes; he lied.)
2. **Cassie's brother accidentally broke Mom's favorite plant when he was carefully getting a ball that she had thrown in the garden.** (No.)
3. **Diedre ate Twinkies her mom told her not to.** (Yes, disobeyed parent.)

If we do something wrong, we can ask God for forgiveness. Always

keep 1 John 1:9 in mind. (Read verse aloud.) **In that passage, God says I am clean after I confess my sin in prayer, so I don't need to feel guilty anymore. I should apologize if I wronged someone.** Have kids finish stories 1 and 3 above in a positive way.

> **OPTIONAL ACTIVITY**
>
> **Prayer**
> Write 1 John 1:9 on a chalkboard. Divide kids into three groups. Group 1 repeats in chorus, "If we confess our sins." Second group repeats, "He is faithful and just and will forgive us our sins." Third group: "and purify us from all unrighteousness." Have them repeat it several times. Then have Group 1 say, "If we confess," and pause for two minutes for kids to substitute one thing about which they feel guilt now in a silent prayer; then you point to Groups 2 and 3 to say their phrases.

STEP 4

NOBODY KNOWS BUT JESUS
Bible Writing

When you feel down, do you ever feel as though no one understands? Recall the skit and how each thought her situation was the worst and no one understood the others.

One person does understand how you feel, and that's Jesus. Let's look at some of the experiences that gave Him good reason to feel awful.

Provide kids with pencils and paper. Have the following verses ready to read, one at a time. Tell them you'll give them 30 seconds to write down the reason Jesus felt sorrowful or disappointed. (Ideas are given in parentheses.)
John 1:10 (Jesus was God's Son but most people didn't recognize Him.)
John 15:18 (The world hated Jesus.)
Matthew 27:27-31 (People made fun of Jesus, spat on Him, and hit Him.)
John 7:3-5 (He ws rejected by His own brothers.)

Quickly go over the answers. Then, say something like **Jesus' sorrows and disappointments were serious because He was God and the Creator of the world. So, imagine how awful to have people not recognize Him, to desert Him, try to kill Him.**

Conclude by pointing out that Jesus understands because, like some of us, he was made fun of, mistreated, and not accepted. Explain that He not only understands how we feel; He wants to help us with our sorrow. Read Matthew 11:28. Explain that we can tell Him how we feel and why, and that He will help us find ways to get over our sadness and deal with the problem that's causing it.

STEP 5

HOW DO THEY RATE?
Rating Sad Times

Refer again to the list on the chalkboard from Step 2. Have kids walk up and add other things to the list that make them sad.

Decide how to rate experiences in order of "very Serious (1); pretty serious (2), not so serious (3)"—though sometimes a "3" for one person is a "2" or "1" for another. Point out that it's important to figure out exactly why you do feel bad. And it takes longer to get over a 1 than a 3—though sometimes a "3" for one person is a "2" or a "1" for another.

STEP 6

THINGS TO DO WHEN I FEEL AWFUL
Idea Sheet

Give kids time to do reproducible sheet 5-B: "Things to Do When I Feel in the Pits." When they are finished, have them share their lists. End the session by pointing out that everyone should have "Tell Jesus in prayer" on their list because it's God who can change the way we see things and, as a result, we'll feel better. Be sure to point out that the "Special Reminder" at the end of the idea list is for everyone.

Close by offering to be the adult to whom kids can come anytime.

IDEAS FOR EXPANDING THIS LESSON

Plan a "funny" party in which everyone does something to make the others laugh. They may want to tell jokes, do impersonations, read something they've read or written, pantomime to a recording. (You may want to preview their "acts" in advance.) Be sure kids understand that laughter is one of God's provisions for cheering ourselves up.

S·K·I·T

Kid #2 is sitting sadly in a chair. Kid #1 enters the room, slumps, and looks miserable.

Kid #1: What a rotten day. I study for hours for the math exam and then fail it anyway. That's going to give me a failing grade!

Kid #2: You think that's bad. I wrecked my bike yesterday and my dad's making me pay for it. I'll have to work for nothing forever!

They sit, head on hands, sighing and groaning.

Kid #3 enters. He also sits, looks sad, and stares at the floor.

Kid #1: Wait until I tell you what happened to me!

Kid #2: Never mind him. Let me tell you about what happened to *me*.

Kid #3: It can't be as bad as what happened to me. The dog got my baseball card collection and chewed it to pieces!

Kids #1 and 2 don't answer. They just keep looking down and moaning and sighing. Kid #3 looks at them frowning as though he doesn't understand what's the matter with them. Kid #4 enters.

Kid #4: Wait till you hear the awful thing that happened to me today—

Kids #1, 2, and 3 get up quickly, wave their hands disgustedly at him, and stomp out, leaving kid #4 sitting alone and looking confused.

THINGS·TO·DO WHEN I FEEL DOWN

Instructions: Make a list of things to do when you feel very sad or disappointed. Here are some ideas to choose from:

Tell Jesus in prayer exactly what's wrong and how I feel. Cry if I want to. Ask God to help me.

Get exercise by going swimming, bike riding, running or walking, skateboarding, or playing another sport.

Tell someone who's mature and whom I trust, just how I feel, and ask for help.

Call or visit a friend who makes me laugh.

Listen to upbeat music.

Get a joke book from the library.

Watch a funny TV show.

Write thoughts in a notebook.

Make a list of things I have to be happy about.

Help someone worse off than myself; maybe mow an elderly person's lawn.

Important: If the miseries don't go away in two weeks, tell a responsible adult that you need help.

God's Plan for the Sexes
or, Christians and Homosexuality

• KEY CONCEPT

Sex between people of the same gender is forbidden in Scripture, but healthy friendships between those of the same gender are part of God's plan.

• SCRIPTURES

1 Samuel 18:1-4; Romans 1:24-27; Genesis 2:21-24

• GOALS

General: Students will understand key factors about homosexuality: what it is and isn't, and God's view of it.
Specific: Students will be able to

A. understand that God created man and woman to be sexual partners
B. explain that Scripture describes homosexual acts as sinful, but God loves the homosexual
C. understand that a close relationship with a friend of the same sex doesn't mean we are homosexual

• BACKGROUND

This lesson: Homosexuality isn't the easiest subject to talk about, but it certainly is something kids need to hear about from a Christian perspective. With the media full of the subject and TV shows presenting it to kids as "an alternative lifestyle," and with books in public libraries doing the same thing, Christian educators cannot afford to avoid it.

Kids at this age are developing their sexuality, are curious, and often experiment with sex—and that may include doing so with kids of their own gender. Unscrupulous people may take advantage of kids at this stage and try to convince them that if they've been attracted at all to the same sex, they are homosexual and should pursue that lifestyle. It's up to us to present the subject from a biblical perspective.

Gary Collins writes, "It is tragic to observe the condemnation and horror with which so many Christians react to homosexuality. Growing up in such an environment, young people learn to fear homosexuals and to suppress any gay tendencies within themselves instead of dealing with them. If these tendencies persist, the young person keeps them hidden. . . . By its condemning attitude, therefore, the church sometimes pushes people into situations in which overt homosexual behavior is encouraged" (Gary R. Collins, *Christian Counseling*, Word, 1980; p. 328).

For your further study:
You may feel uncomfortable teaching a lesson on homosexuality, but reading

on the subject and discussing it with informed Christian peers will help put you at ease.

Christian Counseling by Gary R. Collins (Word, 1980) has a helpful chapter, titled "Homosexuality."

• PREPARATION

1. Have pencils, two papers, and a Bible for each child.
2. Have a chalkboard available.
3. Cut up one copy of reproductible sheet 6-A.
4. Pray for sensitivity on your part to this subject, and that your kids will understand it, and if any have been involved they will seek forgivenss.
For alternative and optional activities (see below):
Copy enough of reproducible sheet 6-A for each child to have one.

STEP 1

GUYS AND GALS
Pairing-off Game

Form students into two teams and distribute men's names from sheet 6-A to team A and women's names to team B. Each person is to carry the name in full view. Allow up to five minutes for the famous couples to find each other. If your class is large, students without names can act as "matchmakers." Afterward, make sure they are paired correctly, and introduce them. (Correct couples: George Washington and Martha; Johnny Cash and June; Prince Charles and Diana; Abraham Lincoln and Mary; Abraham and Sarah; Adam and Eve; Billy Graham and Ruth; Fred Flintstone and Wilma; Cinderella and Prince Charming; Richard Nixon and Pat; George Bush and Barbara; Mikhail Gorbachev and Raisa.)

Point out that from the beginning of creation, men and women have been getting married, having sex, and establishing a family life. Read aloud Genesis 2:21-24. **That's God's plan—for intimate relations to take place between a man and woman who are married, though not every person will marry of course. It seems pretty obvious that men and women are made for one another. So why are we talking about it? Because very different ideas are being presented these days, and we need to understand what they are and how they relate to us.**

Alternative Approach
Students match husbands with wives on the activity sheet. Give the answers listed above.

STEP 2

GUYS AND GUYS AND GALS AND GALS
Unscrambling Words

Write the following news story on the chalkboard. Explain that the words that have to do with homosexuality are scrambled. Provide pencil and paper and allow about five minutes for them to unscramble the words.

Somhoexual, both ygas and beslain, marched through the city today. They carried signs that said, "Rosetehuaxsl are unfair. Our xlause ferpernece is our own business. Homosexuality is an evritaletan yeltsefil."
(Answers: gays, homosexual, lesbian, heterosexuals, sexual preference, alternative lifestyle.)

After giving answers, read a definition of one of the words from the list below and ask kids to assign it to one of the words in the story. Provide correct answers. Be sure kids understand the definitions.

Someone who desires to have sex with a person of his or her own gender; boys with boys, girls with girls (homosexual).

Another word for homosexual (gay).

Women who desire to have sex with other women (lesbian).

When it refers to homosexuality this word refers to choosing to have sexual relations with persons of one's own gender (alternative lifestyle).

Someone with a sexual desire for those of the opposite sex (heterosexual).

Whether one likes male or female as a sexual partner; it's considered by some simply a matter of personal taste, not of right and wrong (sexual preference).

Say that **some homosexuals insist that there's nothing sinful about having sex with another guy if you're a guy or with a girl if you're a girl. They have parades carrying signs that say so and that anyone who thinks differently is prejudiced. These homosexuals want to be accepted as though they were husband and wife.**

Alternative Approach

You may choose to unscramble the words in the news story together or have kids work in small groups and share their answers with the whole group.

STEP 3

WRITE THE REAL STORY
Bible Lesson

Provide pencil and paper and divide into small groups. Explain that we are newspaper reporters assigned to write a story describing God's view of homosexuality. **We are going to do the research for our story now. A newspaper reporter has to answer the questions of who, what, when, where, how, and why when he writes. Your groups are to go over the Scripture and answer together these questions I'm going to write on the chalkboard. That's the research you'll do so you can write a story for the evening edition. Look at Romans 1:24-27 while I'm writing.**

Write the following questions on the chalkboard.

1. Who is the authority you are quoting in your story?
2. What does God say about homosexual activities?
3. What words especially tell how God sees homosexuality?
4. When are homosexual acts wrong—in Bible times or today too? Cities where Bible people lived or everywhere?
5. How has God acted because some people insist on performing homosexual acts?
6. Why is homosexuality sinful?

Conclude by summarizing key points. Say that God calls homosexual activities wrong, but He loves the homosexual himself.

Alternative Approach

To save time, have kids look up the Scripture, and then instead of writing the questions on the chalkboard, read them aloud. Give time to decide on an answer and write it down.

STEP 4

PICTURE THIS
Illustrating

See that each person has pencil and paper. Say that to accompany the newspaper story we'll want a photograph of a wedding. Ask each student to draw one. Show what they've drawn. Re-read Genesis 2:21-24 and discuss how a wedding relates to it.

STEP 5

WHAT'S TRUE AND WHAT'S NOT
A Game

Divide into two teams. The team "up to bat" stands (Team B first). Team A makes a statement that is either true or false about any subject (e.g., "Fluoride helps prevent cavities." True. "German shepherd is a kind of cat." False.) Member on Team B must answer "True" or "False" within five seconds. Some statements may be silly like "Grass is blue." The game will be fun if a fast pace is kept up so as to throw your opponent off guard. A wrong answer disqualifies a player. When all on Team A have had a turn, teams reverse roles. The team with the most players left standing wins.

Afterward say something like this: **It's important to know what's true. Sometimes truth is obvious** (use one of their questions to illustrate). **Sometimes it's not, because different people say different things. That's why it's important to go to the source of the truth. As we've seen, the truth about the wrongness of homosexual acts is found in the Bible.**

OPTIONAL ACTIVITY

Review
Together, using information from Step 3, have kids tell things they'd include in a news story based on Romans 1:24-27. List ideas on chalkboard.

STEP 6

WHAT ABOUT BROTHERLY LOVE?
A Discussion

Many of us have best friends we like to be with. We eat together at school, walk home together, talk to one another on the phone, go places together. We care about one another.

Two young men who had that kind of friendship were David and Jonathan. Read 1 Samuel 18:1, 3, 4.

How did Jonathan feel about David? (Loved him as himself.)

How did Jonathan and David show their love? (Made a covenant. Explain that a covenant is an agreement. They agreed to take care of each other. They also gave each other things that were important to them.)

Tell this story: **Carrie's best friend was Marcia. They saw each other every day and often stayed overnight at one another's house. When a kid at school said Carrie was weird because she was so close to Marcia,**

she felt terrible. Did that mean there was something wrong with her? (Of course not. They were loving friends.) **Jesus himself had close relationships with some of the men He knew, such as Lazarus and three of His disciples: Peter, James, and John.**

Please note: Some of the boys and girls in your group may have experimented with sex with members of their own gender. They feel extremely guilty about it and wonder if that means they're homosexual. Before you close in prayer, invite kids who have questions to stay and talk to you. Point out that any sin they may have committed can be forgiven.

IDEAS FOR EXPANDING THIS LESSON

Invite a Christian counselor to discuss this subject in a way appropriate for this age group.

Husbands	Wives
George Washington	Sarah
Johnny Cash	Cinderella
Prince Charles	Raisa
Abraham Lincoln	Diana
Abraham	Wilma
Adam	Martha
Billy Graham	Pat
Fred Flintstone	Mary
Prince Charming	Barbara
Richard Nixon	Ruth
George Bush	June
Mikhail Gorbachev	Eve

It's My Turn Now
or, Taking the Initiative to Change the Things I Can

• KEY CONCEPT

God gives us the ability to take the initiative to make things better.

• SCRIPTURES

Genesis 1:1-5, 2:15; Exodus 31:1-6; Proverbs 6:6-11; John 3:16; Galatians 5:19-23; 6:7-10; Matthew 6:10

• GOALS

General: The students will explore their God-given creativity which they can use to help His will be done.

Specific: Students will be able to

A. see that God isn't just "there"; He is active doing things
B. see that God gives us power and freedom to accomplish new things, with responsibility to do them according to what He wants
C. explore ways they can take initiative
D. plan to do something they've been putting off, or finish something they've started

• BACKGROUND

This lesson: The "Serenity Prayer" says: "Lord, give me the serenity to accept the things I cannot change, the courage to change the things I can, and the wisdom to know the difference." Those are Biblical concepts. While the Bible tells us to thank God in all circumstances (1 Thessalonians 5:18) and patiently endure trials (James 5:10-11), it also urges us to take the initiative to put our faith into action (James 2:14-26) and make the most of every opportunity (Colossians 4:5).

God the Creator, who made everything and will someday make all things new (Revelation 21:5), puts a spark of His creative energy into every person. It's the source of art and invention. It makes human beings experiment, risk, fiddle, revise, and generally want to change the way things are. In younger children, creativity flows naturally, but when kids reach the age of your students, creativity may be stifled—by certain mass entertainment, by unimaginative schools, by the kids' desire to imitate their peers, and perhaps even by church programs which aim to produce a certain predictable kind of kid.

Today's lesson is on taking the initiative in life: daring to go ahead and imagine and search out new solutions to stumping problems. When we take initiative under God's direction, we're His coworkers doing His work in the world. Kids ages eight to twelve may be skeptical that they can have any effect on anything. Though they're increasingly independent, they will feel very restricted and defined by the rules of family, school, and church. But they should feel secure enough to start and finish things on their own within the safe boundaries of those restrictions. They can accomplish things for God, exceeding their own and adults' expectations of them.

• PREPARATION

1. Gather pencils for everyone.
2. Have available an ordinary, familiar object which has a specific use, such as a toothbrush, pen, wrench, mirror, or shoelace. Your students will be inventing new uses for it. In case they get stuck or are inhibited, you should think of a *really* far-out use for it and be prepared to demonstrate.
3. Provide at least 20 sheets of construction paper or other paper, five or more markers or crayons, and tape and scissors.
4. Make a copy of reproducible sheets 7-A and 7-B for each student.
5. Have at least two Bibles available.
6. Pray that God's Spirit will encourage your kids to take the initiative to do the right things.
For alternative and optional activities (see below):
For the alternative approach to Step 1, you'll need a sheet of paper for each team.

STEP 1

AN ORDINARY OBJECT?
Exercising Creativity

Take the ordinary object you brought and pass it around the group. As the object is passed to each student, he or she should invent a new use for the object, and demonstrate. (Example: use a toothbrush for erasing the blackboard.) The crazier the use, the more fun! If a student can't think of something within a certain time limit, such as 10 seconds, the object is passed to the next person; there'll be another chance when it comes around again. If students have trouble getting started, or if their new uses for the object are kind of dull, demonstrate the crazy use *you've* thought of! Keep passing the object around until ideas begin to be exhausted.

Did it surprise you that you could come up with so many different new ways to use this? Did it help to hear the ideas other people came up with? What did you have to do to think of new ways to use this? After some discussion, point out: To come up with new ways to use this, you had to go ahead and think and then do something. You couldn't just sit there and stare at it with your mind turned off. You had to put your mind to work to come up with an idea, then you had to put your body into action to show us the idea in your mind.

Alternative Approach
Divide into teams, show them the object you've brought, and have a competition to see how many new uses for the object they can write down within a certain time limit. Each team reads their list aloud. The other team or teams can challenge any of the ideas. If challenged, team members must demonstrate using the object that way.

OPTIONAL ACTIVITY

Sharing Stories
Ask students to briefly share any "initiation" activities they have ever been involved in. Not all kids this age have had this experience; be prepared to tell a bit about your college initiation days or something.

STEP 2

WHAT'S IT MEAN?
Defining Initiative

Are any of you wearing something with your initials on it? Do you have anything with you that has your initials on it? "Initial" and the words related to "initial" mean first or beginning. Your "initial" is the letter which begins your name. An "initiation" is something you do when people first join a club.

Any time we go ahead and start something new, instead of being lazy about it or letting somebody else do it, that's called "taking initiative." What are some things you've initiated—in other words, things you've done on your own? If students don't understand or can't think of things right away, ask: **What are some things you've made?** (For example: woodworking projects, models, drawings) **What are some things you've made up?** (Songs, games, stories.)

Distribute reproducible sheet 7-A, "Start Something!" and have kids fill it out.

Ask them to share some of their answers. Affirm the many ways your kids have already initiated good things in their lives.

STEP 3

GOD THE CREATOR
Seeing God's Creativity

The reason we can take initiative and do things that make a difference in the world is that God put that ability into us. He's the One who first started everything. He's the Creator, which means He made everything there is. Sometimes people picture God as just sitting on a throne in heaven with angels singing all around Him—He's not really doing anything. But God *does* things.

Read Genesis 1:1-5. It's only the beginning of the story of the creation, but it shows God taking action in a big way. If kids ask questions such as "What were things like before God made the world?" or "Why did He decide to do that?" you can congratulate them for asking deep questions and admit that nobody knows, but we *do* know that He took the initiative to make everything.

God didn't stop doing things when He was finished making the world. All along through human history He has done things in our world, and the greatest (summed up in John 3:16) is when He sent Christ to die for us. Read John 3:16. **And God still isn't finished doing things. Someday when Christ returns He'll make everything perfect again. Meanwhile, He takes the initiative to do things in our lives every day. What are some things God does for us?** (Guides us, provides for our needs such as food and homes, gives us loving family and friends, teaches us to get along with each other, helps us obey Him, forgives us.)

Alternative Approach
If you're running short on time, or if you need more activity for your kids, help your kids just quickly list out loud things God does and did, and skip the rest of Step 3.

STEP 4

MANKIND THE MAKER
Seeing Mankind's Creativity

From the beginning, as soon as He made mankind, God also gave us things to do. Read Genesis 2:15. **Adam wasn't supposed to just sit in the garden and enjoy it; he had a job to do there. Later, when God told Moses to build the tabernacle or tent of worship, He gave people special skills to do the job right.** Read Exodus 31:1-6.

God has given each of us abilities and skills which He wants us to go ahead and use. Read Proverbs 6:6-11. Explain if necessary that a "sluggard" is a lazy person, "provisions" are food, and "scarcity" means not having enough for your daily needs.

Give kids construction paper, markers, and scissors. Working together as a class, make a large ant. Then, on the "ant" have kids write their answers to these questions: **What does the ant take the initiative to do? How should people imitate ants? What happens if we don't take initiative?** Tape your completed ant onto your wall. It would be nice to give it a name.

Have students look again at their sheet "Start Something!" to see some of the ways they have already followed the example of the ant. Let them add more examples as they've thought of them. Encourage them in the positive ways they are already taking initiative to make things better.

Alternative Approach
If you have a large class, different groups can work on different sections of the ant and assemble them later.

STEP 5

DON'T GIVE UP
Deciding to Keep Obeying the Lord

Like a lot of other things, our God-given creativity can be used in wrong ways as well as right ways. A person could be as busy as an ant while out stealing or spreading lies or disobeying parents. That's using our God-given initiative in the wrong ways. Read Galatians 6:7-10. **We have a responsibility to take the initiative with things that the Lord wants, not other things. This Scripture encourages us not to give up on doing good.**

All of us have given up sometimes when things didn't work out the way we wanted. There are times when we need to accept things as they are. But often, with just a bit more creativity and work and a lot of faith in the Lord, we can change things if we'll only keep at it.

What help do these verses in Galatians 6 give us for deciding which things we should give up on and what we should try a little harder on? (Galatians 5:19-23 will also help.)

Take a moment to pray the Lord's Prayer together . Then point out Matthew 6:10. **We've all prayed for the Lord's will to be done on earth. By taking initiative and going ahead and doing what he wants, we're being part of the answer to our prayer.**

Distribute reproducible sheet 7-B, "Changing What I Can," and ask students to fill out the multiple-choice part at the top. Discuss how you might take the right kind of initiative in these situations. Think of other situations—at home, at school, at church, other places.

Now ask students to complete the last two statements by writing or drawing something they need to get started with, and something they've put off completing and need to finish. Discuss how you can help each other accomplish these new goals of taking the initiative.

IDEAS FOR EXPANDING THIS LESSON

Discuss something your class can do or make or perform for your church. It could be anything from a skit to a song to practical help such as handing out the bulletins one Sunday. What's important is that your class initiates the project and carries it through. It will give your kids tremendous new confidence in what they can do in the Lord, and it will demonstrate to adults that your kids have much to offer the church.

God gives all of us the ability to INITIATE (go ahead and start) things. You've probably TAKEN THE INITIATIVE a lot more than you think! For example:

What are some jobs you've gone ahead and done at home without being asked?

THAT'S TAKING INITIATIVE!

Who are some new friends you've made because you took the time to be friendly and get to know them?

THAT'S TAKING INITIATIVE!

What's something you've learned to do just because you wanted to, not because it was assigned in school?

THAT'S TAKING INITIATIVE!

What's something you've built or made just for the fun and challenge of it?

THAT'S TAKING INITIATIVE!

If I don't like something, I usually:

____ complain
____ keep my mouth shut
____ throw a tantrum
____ try to reason with whoever's in charge

If I see something unfair being done to somebody, I usually:

____ pretend I didn't see it
____ cheer
____ beat up the guilty person
____ stick up for the underdog

If a family member told me to do something that wasn't God's will, I think I would:

____ do it
____ try to reason with the person
____ suggest something else
____ avoid doing it
____ tell the person "no" and explain why

Here's something new I'm going to *do:*

free! helpful hints:

- look in my closet for unfinished projects
- look in my homework for unfinished assignments
- is there somebody I need to forgive and I haven't quite done it?
- is there somebody I need to tell "I'm sorry" and I haven't gotten around to saying it?

Here's something I've started and have been putting off finishing, and I'm going to *finish:*

In Their Shoes
or, Helping a Friend by Showing Compassion

- **KEY CONCEPT** When a friend is hurting, we should listen and feel their hurt with them.
- **SCRIPTURES** John 11:33-36
- **GOALS** **General:** Students will see an example of Jesus' compassion and understand the importance of feeling with the person who is hurting.
Specific: Students will
  A. see the importance of standing with a hurting person
  B. list and discuss some wrong responses to a hurting friend
  C. learn and practice active listening
- **BACKGROUND** **This lesson:** Your friend's child died. You feel terrible when you hear the news. You want to say the "right thing." But when you see them, you just don't bring it up. It's too hard to know what to say, what to do. You might mumble an embarrassed sympathy or send a card, but what do you *say?* We prefer to be confronted with situations we can fix. We want to offer quick advice or easy answers. It's confusing when suddenly we face a situation with no explanation or solution. How do you explain God's role in it? How do you offer hope to the hurting person? We can even get to the point where, when we see that person coming, we head the other way, just because we're embarrassed at our futility in the situation. Yet when Jesus went to Bethany, He went *after* Lazarus' death, when all human hope was gone. And when he met Mary, He didn't say, "Guess what, Mary? I'm the Son of God, so I can raise him from the dead! Don't cry—I'll make everything better!" Instead He just stood there and cried with her. His deepest insides were torn apart at her grief, even though He knew Lazarus was coming to life in a few minutes. It doesn't seem very logical, but it sure paints an incredible picture of what real compassion is all about! Even the critical onlookers, who usually critiqued everything that Jesus did, were amazed! They commented, "He must have loved him!"

We're just human. We can never feel for another as selflessly as Jesus could. But we can take our cue from Him, and at least try to step into our hurting friend's shoes for a moment. We can cry and listen and pray. And they will know we care about them.

For your further study: If you have extra time, consider looking at *How to Help a Friend* by Paul Welter (Tyndale, 1978).

- **PREPARATION**

1. Have a blackboard, large paper, or overhead available.
2. Provide blindfolds for half the children in your class (if unavailable, plan on asking your most honest children to close their eyes).
3. Make a list of about 10 objects in your classroom which could be identified by touch. Make copies for half your class.
4. Make enough copies of sheet 8-A for half your class.
5. Pray that your kids will start developing compassion for each other.

For alternative and optional activities (see below):

Provide enough construction paper for each student to have at least one piece.

Provide one piece of aluminum foil for each student.

Make sure you have enough markers/pens and scissors for everyone.

Provide pens/pencils and plain papers for each student.

STEP 1

TRUST WALK
A Game

As students arrive, pair them up. Make sure you pair up children who will work well together, but won't clown around too much. Have one of each pair blindfolded (or if necessary tell that child to keep his eyes tightly closed). Give the seeing person the list of objects in your classroom. When you give the signal, the seeing partners must lead their blindfolded partners to all of those objects. The seeing partners cannot talk except to say "yes" when their blindfolded partner correctly guesses what the object is. The seeing partners can guide their blindfolded partner's hands to important parts of the unknown object quickly. The goal is to be the first couple to identify all of the objects on the list.

Discuss these as a group afterward:

How did the seeing person help the blindfolded person?

Were they giving lots of advice?

Did they say things like, "Why can't you see this?"

Sometimes when a friend is in trouble, we wonder what's wrong with them. We need to step into their shoes and walk with them. They need to feel that we are there with them, ready to guide them toward help, but not offering too much advice or just telling them to stop hurting. That wouldn't really help.

STEP 2

WAS JESUS COMPASSIONATE?
Reading a Bible Story

Let me tell you a story. Jesus had some friends who lived in Bethany. Two sisters and a brother. One day the brother, Lazarus, died. When Jesus came, one of Lazarus' sisters came to meet him. The Bible says, read John 11:33-36.

Even though Jesus knew that He could solve the problem, He felt so sad to see His friends hurting that He cried. And He didn't just cry, He was "deeply moved in spirit and troubled." This is the deepest compassion you can give someone—to stand beside them and to cry with them. It was obvious to all the people around them that Jesus loved Lazarus. The Jews said, "See how He loved him!"

STEP 3

GOOF!
Acting Out the Wrong Response

Were you ever hurt or sad, and someone came along and made you feel even worse? Divide the class into pairs again. In the pairs, have them act out a friend talking to Mary. One of them is to be Mary, hurting over Lazarus' death, while the other is to demonstrate a response that doesn't help. Give them about five minutes to run through these role plays. During this time, wander around and watch the different responses.

As a group, list the wrong responses you thought of for when a friend is hurting. Use your blackboard, overhead, or large piece of paper to record these. Hopefully, they will come up with ideas like "give lots of advice, tell the person they shouldn't feel bad, label that person, command them." If they are having trouble, you might act out one of these wrong responses and see if they can identify it.

Think how Mary would have responded if Jesus had said, "Oh, come on, Mary. Just go home and fix yourself a cup of tea. Everyone has to die sometime!" Fortunately, Mary had Jesus for a friend and not one of us. And even though He could fix her hurting, He still stopped to cry with her!

OPTIONAL ACTIVITY

A Shoe Game

Play this if your kids *don't* have their best shoes on, and if your class is small enough to supervise closely.

We can't just walk up to a friend who is hurting and start crying, though. We have to know what is wrong and we have to be able to feel with them—to understand a little of how they must be feeling. It's like stepping into their shoes to feel their pain.

Have everyone take off their shoes and put them at one end of the room, all mixed up. When all the shoes are there, they are to each find two different shoes and put them on. Supervise to make sure no shoes are being stretched out or otherwise hurt. Then they go find the people wearing the mates of the shoes on their feet. They stand together, left feet with right feet. Pretty soon the whole class should be standing stretched around the room with matched up shoes. Once they have all matched their shoes, say, **The most important way to be able to help your friend who is hurting is to picture yourself standing in their shoes, even if it is uncomfortable or you have to stretch out a bit.**

Then have them take off the shoes, find their own, and sit down.

STEP 4

LEND AN EAR
Practicing Active Listening

Sometimes you can help a hurting friend by giving them something they need, like lending them a jacket if they're shivering. But in other situa-

tions, a hurting friend will just need to talk about whatever is bothering them. When they want to talk, you can be a great listener by doing something called *active listening.* You listen to what your friend says, and then try to "get into their shoes" in your mind so that you can understand what they're feeling. For example, if I say, "I'd like to be in the school play, but I know I'd forget my part, and the audience would laugh at me," what am I feeling? (Unsure of my performing ability.)

So, you might say—using active listening—"You must feel nervous about performing in front of everyone." Then I might go on to explain more of how I was feeling. This would help you to understand my situation well, and it would help me to be able to talk about it. You want to be a mirror for me, to reflect back my feelings to me. Be sure your children understand how this is done.

Have students pick a partner to work with. Pass out sheet 8-A to each pair. They should take turns reading a statement to their partner. The partner reflects back to them the feeling behind the statement (hints are in parentheses). They then switch so that the other partner can do the reflecting. Switch back and forth until all four practice statements are reflected.

These reflections might seem easy, but they can help your friend as you step into his shoes and hurt with him.

Alternative Approach

Have students make mirrors out of construction paper and aluminum foil. Have them think of a statement like, "My brother never plays with me!" or "Why can't I have a puppy like Mark does?" (If it is too hard for your class to generate statements about a hurtful situation, provide them with such statements.) Have them write the statement on the back of the mirror, and then "reflect" the feeling for the statement in the mirror by writing the feeling on construction paper and gluing it on the mirror. Examples of "reflections": "I feel sad because my brother doesn't want to be with me," or "I feel jealous of Mark's good time with his puppy."

OPTIONAL ACTIVITY

Have students privately spend a few minutes thinking of anyone they know who is really hurting. Pass out pieces of paper and pens. Have them write down one way that they can actively listen or get into that person's shoes to feel with him this week. Have them silently, individually pray about this person and his hurt.

STEP 5

HELP ME INTO THESE SHOES
Praying

Pray, asking God to help each of you be willing to deeply care, stepping into a friend's shoes.

IDEAS FOR EXPANDING THIS LESSON

Develop more active listening exercises and practice together.
Keep logs of "goofs" made in listening to others during the week.
Roleplay ways to respond with compassion.

"Will you stay with me when I go to the hospital?"

(Feeling afraid)

"I hate our house! I can never get my homework done there because there's so much noise!"

(Feeling frustrated)

"He thinks he can tell me what to do just because he's on the football team!"

(Feeling inferior about not being on the team)

"Did you see that guy pick up all those weights? Wow! He's strong!"

(Feeling that strength is good)

An Evening of Drama
or, Ideas for a Miniseries Using Lessons 9–11 on the Church

Here are ideas for using lessons 9–11 on the Church for a dramatic evening (in more ways than one) put on for friends and family.

Invite your friends and families and start getting ready weeks in advance for a dramatic production that involves church history, along with some glimpses at symbols in the church and explanations of what the church is.

Here is your "script." Assign the parts ahead of time, of course. You will need seven narrators, Roman citizens, Nero, Roman soldiers, Nicene readers, Stephen and other Children's Crusade kids, sailors, Muslims, John Huss, three Martin Luther storytellers. Double up on parts if necessary.

NARRATOR 1: **The church. We've all heard about it. But what is it, really?**

Well, there are different meanings. It can just mean a building, even. But we're talking now about the people in a church. Many of us go to a particular church, but God has more people than just those who go to our church. The whole, or universal, church is all of God's people. Our leader is Jesus Christ, and He has given us jobs to do, like telling others about Him and helping each other through life. He has given us special abilities to help each other. He has also given the church special symbols to help us understand and remember what He has done for us, like the bread and the cup in the Lord's Supper.

(OPTIONAL: HAVE A COMMUNION SERVICE AT THIS POINT IF YOU WISH. BE SURE TO COMPLY WITH YOUR CHURCH'S "REGULATIONS" ABOUT THIS: E.G., SOME CHURCHES ONLY ALLOW ORDAINED MINISTERS TO SERVE COMMUNION.)

The church has been around for a long, long time. Get comfortable and think with us about some very exciting things that have happened to the church.

NARRATOR 2: **It was the last half of the first century, about 60 years after Jesus was born. Most of the New Testament was already written.**

The church, God's people, was growing. Not because it was exactly a nice group to be a part of—I mean, it was *dangerous* to be a Christian then. In fact, I think you'll agree after this meeting that it usually has been dangerous to be a Christian.

For example, around A.D. 64, there was a bad fire in the city of Rome. (HAVE KIDS ACT THIS OUT AS A TABLEAU BEHIND THE NARRATOR. CAN HAVE NERO IN A WHITE SHEET PLAYING A VIOLIN, AS THE TRADITION GOES.) **Rome was the capital city of one of the most important groups of nations in history, called the Roman Empire. The head of the Roman Empire then, the emperor, was Nero. He decided to blame the Christians for starting the fire! Lots of people believe Nero set the fire himself!**

And Nero didn't just blame them; he had them killed. (HAVE SOL-

DIERS ENTER TABLEAU AND GRAB "CHRISTIANS.") **And he didn't just have them killed; he had them tortured and killed in awful ways like burning and being eaten by dogs and being crucified.**

Many Roman emperors did things like this to the Christians. In fact, thousands of Christians died, and the persecution lasted for over 200 years (TABLEAU ENDS.)

NARRATOR 3: **Then something happened in A.D. 311. A man named Constantine became the emperor. There's a story that he saw in the sky a cross on fire with words written on it that said "By this, conquer." That was just before an important battle which he won. After that Constantine not only stopped any persecution of Christians, but he gave Christians great honor. Christians got the leadership jobs in the empire. The church became very rich.**

Sounds like a very nice change, huh? Well, it certainly was. But then some people said they were Christians just so they could get the better jobs, and they didn't know Jesus. And then Constantine decided he would be the leader of the church, and didn't seem to remember that Jesus is the only King of the church. Eventually men called popes felt they could tell the church and countries what to do. A lot of people started teaching things that did not agree with the Bible. There was one big meeting at a place called Nicea that came up with a paper that a lot of people read in churches even today. It's called the Nicene Creed, and it was written because some people were teaching that Jesus is not God. (Have some students read the creed out loud from reproducible sheet 11-A.)

There were several church elders who helped people learn what God said about important things in the Bible. Some famous ones were Ambrose and Augustine and Jerome.

Something else happened around then when people saw the problems in the church. Some people felt they could please God by getting into small groups and living away from the rest of the world. This is called the beginning of monasticism. Many monks and nuns from this type of living helped keep books that would have been lost, and they helped the poor and sick.

NARRATOR 4: **Meanwhile a big religion was getting started called Islam. Its followers even created a larger empire than the Roman Empire, called the Mohammedan or Muslim Empire. One of its leaders, Caliph Omar, destroyed the world's most famous library because he felt the Muslim "Bible" called the Koran was the only book needed in the world! Thousands of Christian churches were destroyed or made into mosques, where Muslims worship their god Allah. This is still a very big religion in the world.**

Meanwhile more was going on in the church. Back then England was a pretty wild place, and missionaries went to it and told people about Jesus. Some of the most famous were Boniface and Patrick—the one connected with St. Patrick's Day.

Anyway, back to the Muslims. Hundreds of knights and thousands of soldiers went on the Crusades. There were fierce people known as the Turks who took over the land where Jesus used to live, called the Holy Land by many Christians. The Turks became Muslims, and they started

hurting Christians who tried to visit where Jesus used to live. So, many soldiers were sent on the Crusades to try to get the land back in friendly hands. These Crusades took place over hundreds of years! One of the Crusades is a terribly sad story. It's called The Children's Crusade. (HAVE KIDS ACT OUT THE FOLLOWING AS A TABLEAU, WITH STEPHEN TELLING OTHER KIDS AND THE KIDS MARCHING AND SINGING AS INDICATED BELOW, GETTING ON "THE SHIPS," ETC.)

There was a boy named Stephen in France who said that Jesus had appeared to him and told him that He would help children do what so many soldiers and kings had not been able to do. He said that if a lot of kids stood by a sea in France, the water would part before them like it did for Moses. Then they could walk over to the Holy Land. A boy in Germany, named Nicholas, told other kids. And I mean a lot of other kids. Thousands of kids, boys and girls, the average age 12, started to march to meet by the sea in France. As they marched they sang a song. (HAVE THE KIDS AT THIS POINT, THE NARRATOR WAITING, SING THE VERSE OF "FAIREST LORD JESUS" PROVIDED ON REPRODUCIBLE SHEET 11-A.) **You have probably heard of the Alps. They're beautiful but dangerous mountains in Europe, mountains that have snow on them all year round. The kids had to cross them. And many of them died.**

But a lot of them made it to the sea and met the kids from France. Of course, the sea did not open up before them, though.

What could they do? Many went home. But 5,000 stayed. Seven ships offered to take them to the Holy Land, and they got on.

Two of the ships ran into rocks, though, and sank. And something worse, maybe, happened to the kids on the other five ships—the captains turned out to be slave dealers, and they sold the children to Muslims! They never saw their homes again. (END OF TABLEAU.)

NARRATOR 5: **Well, a lot of things were happening in the world then, so many we'd be here all day and night and still not get through the story. But let us simplify it a bit and tell you that the church for the most part was getting farther away from what Jesus taught. It even taught that if you served the church you could get forgiveness for sins, and even if you paid money you could get forgiven! People who tried to teach against the church got into trouble.**

Of course God still cared for His Church, though. Something exciting began to happen that's called the Reformation today, something that helped people learn again how to really get to heaven. Many of its followers were called Protestants. There were people called the Waldensians and men like John Wycliffe who helped people learn what the Bible said. Wycliffe even translated the Bible into the people's language. Copies had to be made by hand; there were still no printing presses. This was in the 1300s.

John Huss is another famous person from this time. He preached about Jesus in the city of Prague, which made many of the church leaders angry. His books were burned in the courtyard of the archbishop's palace. John Huss was asked if he would obey the commands of the pope. This is what John Huss said: (HAVE THE CHILD ASSIGNED THE PART OF JOHN HUSS READ HIS PART ONE FROM THE SCRIPT ON SHEET 11-A. HAVE HIM STAY UP FRONT FOR THE REST OF THIS SCENE.)

Huss was not allowed by the pope to teach in the church anymore. The pope even had the whole city punished until Huss left. But eventually Huss was arrested and placed in a dungeon next to the city sewer! (HAVE "JOHN HUSS" PLUG HIS NOSE.) **He was brought to trial. The sentence was passed: John Huss and his books were to be burned. Huss kneeled down before everyone and prayed out loud:** (HAVE THE CHILD KNEEL DOWN AND READ PART TWO.)

John Huss was led out to die. The priest cried out, "We commit your soul to the devil!" John Huss answered, (HAVE CHILD READ PART THREE). **Then over and over Huss cried,** (HAVE CHILD READ PART FOUR). **The wood and straw were piled up around him even as he still spoke . . . and soon his body was dead.** (HAVE CHILD EXIT.)

There were so many other heroes that we don't have time to tell you about them now. Like Savonarola and Erasmus and Zwingli and Calvin. Let us tell you about two heroes, though, one a group of people and the other a very famous man.

(HAVE THREE STORYTELLERS TELL THE STORY OF MARTIN LUTHER DIVIDED UP FROM REPRODUCIBLE SHEETS 11-B and -C. THEN HAVE EVERYONE SING "A MIGHTY FORTRESS.")

NARRATOR 6: **In France, Protestants were called Huguenots. They actually fought religious wars in France for 30 years against people who did not believe the Bible! The queen mother of France in the late 1500s was Catherine de Medici. She said that it was too bad that the wars were going on, and she said she had a great idea to get a treaty set. She invited all the "important people" of the land to a wedding. The people came and the wedding took place.**

Everybody was celebrating. It was evening. Queen Mother Catherine went to her son, the king, and told him that the Huguenots had formed a plot to kill the entire royal family and the leaders of the Catholics! The king signed a paper that said anyone who wanted to in Paris could kill the Huguenots! The mob went wild; soon thousands of Huguenots were dead.

But guess what? Most of those who were not killed escaped to other countries, and the Huguenots had been among the smartest workers in the entire country of France. A famous writer said that the French leaders had ruined their country in the name of religion.

There were more battles and wars, we're sorry to say. One of the most famous is called the Thirty Years' War in Germany, fought in the 1600s.

Remember how we mentioned England got missionaries when it was wild? Well, by the 1500s England was pretty Christian. But then there was a group called Puritans that felt there had not been enough change for the better. Eventually there were wars in the country over it. Have you ever heard of the story of Pilgrim's Progress? It was written by John Bunyan, who was put in jail for years for preaching without the government's permission! In fact, he wrote it in jail.

NARRATOR 7: **We've not said much about Canada or the United States, have we? Nothing, in fact. This was still a hundred years before America became an independent nation. Many Puritans helped settle America.**

Well, even after all those battles and all those sermons, the Protestant church still had problems. Not with the Catholics, but with itself. There were many people who taught others how they felt they should get to know God better.

There came a time when a lot of Christians in America and England changed a lot, to try to follow God better. Some famous preachers were Jonathan Edwards, John Wesley, and George Whitefield.

We've really not said much about Africa or South America either, have we? Or China and other places. It's because, I'm sorry to say, very, very few Christians ever got there. Finally, in the late 1700s, which was after America was an independent nation, people began to be more interested in helping others know about Jesus in those other countries. Some famous missionaries were William Carey to India, Adoniram Judson to Burma, Robert and Mary Moffat to Africa, James Hudson Taylor to China, and John Paton to the New Hebrides islands. As John Paton was getting ready to leave, he was told by an old man in Scotland, "But the cannibals! You will be eaten by the cannibals!" But God protected him from the warriors and witch doctors, and so many people became Christians that he said "his joy was almost too great to be borne."

So many more things happened, of course, too. The Sunday School a lot like we know it became common for the first time in the 1800s. In the 1900s there were countries taken over by people who did not allow the church to meet, and many Christians were killed and are still being killed. In the free countries many books began to be published which are still being published on hundreds of things about the Bible. And now the world is changing even more. Countries in places like Africa are now sending out many missionaries!

TEACHER: **Christians still don't agree on everything, by any means. God doesn't even say we have to agree on everything. But He's always had people who truly love Him and their neighbor and try to obey what He has given us in the Bible. And even when those people were killed because they loved God, God took care of them and carried them home to heaven. God's enemies cannot stop His church.** (HAVE ALL YOUR KIDS RECITE MATTHEW 16:18.)

Let's all pray and thank God for the wonderful heroes and heroines He has given us in church history, and let's pray that we would be faithful like they were. . . .

Close the evening with refreshments. Here are some ideas:

Have a complete dinner with an international flair. Tie in the dishes with church history—e.g., the Romans adapted Greek cuisine, so serve a Greek salad for an appetizer (with oil and vinegar dressing, feta cheese, and black olives); for dessert serve a classic German dish such as apple strudel.

Have a sandwich bar with lots of ingredients to choose from. Give suggestions for sandwiches that tie in with church history. For example, a sandwich in pita (pocket) bread would remind a kid of a ship in the Children's Crusade.

How's This Monster Work?
or, How the Church Works

part 1 of miniseries
The Church

• KEY CONCEPT

God has formed His church on earth for special reasons, and we organize ourselves a bit to help fulfill those reasons.

• SCRIPTURES

1 Corinthians 1:2; Ephesians 1:22-23; Colossians 1:18; Ephesians 4:15-16; 1 Thessalonians 5:11, 13-15; 1 John 3:16-18; Hebrews 10:24-25; Revelation 1:5-6; James 5:14-15; Matthew 5:14; 28:19-20; Galatians 6:1-2; James 5:19-20; Acts 15; 16:4; 6:1-6; 14:23

• GOALS

General: Each student will understand why the church is here and how it has organized itself to serve God better.
Specific: Students will be able to
A. say what the church is
B. explain some of the major tasks Christ has given His church
C. tell who is the head of the church
D. understand that the church has organized itself in different ways to help itself fulfill the purposes God has given it.
E. explain the basic organization of their local church
F. appreciate the universal church God has made and the individual contributions of their particular church.

• BACKGROUND

This lesson: The church can seem like an unfriendly monster to kids. So many leaders, so much going on, and so few obvious reasons for it all.

Sometimes we have too many leaders, and sometimes we have too much going on. But even healthy churches can seem confusing to kids. This lesson will change all that for your group. Through guided discussion and fun activities, your students will learn what the church is, why it's here, and how your particular church has been organized to help people do what God wants.

Your group may not be affiliated with a church. In that case, you may not find this lesson useful for your group. If you wish to adapt it, however, just stay away from getting real specific on how a particular church is organized.

By the way, if you're interested in helping your kids get involved in your church, see the session "It's My Church" mentioned in the below resources.

For your further study: There is a practical lesson plan on helping your kids with getting involved in church—"It's My Church" in *Friendships Made to Last* in the Kid Builders series (Victor, 1990).

• PREPARATION

1. Gather enough pencils and blank papers for very kid to have one.
2. Tear out reproducible sheet 9-A and cut it in half as marked.
3. Have at least two Bibles available.
4. Gather hymnals or other songbooks for at least half your class to have one.

For alternative and optional activities (see below):

Invite some parents who lead in your church to share how they do that and any frustrations or needs they have in those areas.

Invite a special speaker, such as your pastor or a local seminary student, to speak in a simple way on what your church government is like.

Have someone come in to accompany your group singing on an instrument.

Have extra paper for groups to write down the songs they make up about the church.

STEP 1

WHAT AND WHY IS A CHURCH?

Puzzle-Making

Divide your large group in two and hand out the two halves of reproducible sheet 9-A, along with pencils and blank papers. The sheet lists facts about the church and where we learn those facts in the Bible. Have each group make up puzzles or other games to see if the other group can figure out the facts from the Scripture references with perhaps a few clues. For example, they can list brief clues and verse references to fill in a crossword puzzle. Let them take their time at this.

Then have the groups trade puzzles/games and work on them together. Circulate to make sure everyone seems to be understanding the facts brought out in their puzzles.

Alternative Approaches

If you have a very large class, one that would find it difficult to work together to make one small puzzle, you could cut reproducible sheet 9-A in four pieces for four smaller groups.

If your kids need more competition to keep them interested, offer a prize to the team that makes up the hardest puzzle—the puzzle that's finished last.

STEP 2

WHAT WE'VE DONE ABOUT IT

Discussing

God has given His church important work to do on earth. There are too many of us, and unfortunately we don't get along well enough yet, to meet all together in one humongous church building. So we meet in smaller groups all over the world. And we've organized ourselves to get that work done. For example, most churches have some plan of what's going to happen in their main worship services—someone will speak, songs will be sung, etc.

Do any of you have parents who lead something in our church? Let them share.

Briefly explain to your children how your particular church is run. For example, perhaps you have two pastors, one who does most of the speaking and visitation and one who organizes the Christian education ministries such as youth group and Sunday School, and they have people "under" them who help.

Alternative Approach
If you have time and some willing parents, let parents who lead in your church share with your group what they do and any frustrations or needs they have in those areas.

OPTIONAL ACTIVITY

Special Speaker
Have a special speaker, such as your pastor or a local seminary student, explain in a simple way what your church government is like. For example, they could explain what the elders or the bishops or the deacons in your church do and how they are chosen.

STEP 3

I LOVE YOUR CHURCH
Singing

Hand out hymnals or other songbooks from your church and sing one or more songs about the church, such as "The Church's One Foundation" or "I Love Thy Church, O God."

Close in prayer by going around the room and thanking God for the church and asking Him to make it stronger for His glory.

Alternative Approaches
Have someone accompany your group with an instrument on those songs.
Have small groups make up songs about the church.

IDEAS FOR EXPANDING THIS LESSON

Please see the suggestions just before this lesson for using lessons 9–11 in a series on the church. It includes having a play for other people and winding up with some clever refreshments.

The church is made up of all Christians.

1 Corinthians 1:2

Jesus Christ is the head of the church.

Ephesians 1:22-23; Colossians 1:18

God has given the church gifts for us to use to help each other.

Ephesians 4:15-16

Here are some verses that list some things we're to do to help each other: *1 Thessalonians 5:11, 13-15; 1 John 3:16-18.*

The church has organized itself on earth to help itself do what God wants it to do.

Acts 15

God wants Christians to meet with each other.

Hebrews 10:24-25

Christians are all supposed to pray for and serve each other.

Revelation 1:5-6; James 5:14-15

The church is to be a "light" in the world.

Matthew 5:14; 28:19-20

If another person in the church is having trouble living like a Christian, the others are supposed to help him.

Galatians 6:1-2; James 5:19-20

The church has organized itself on earth to help itself do what God wants it to do.

Acts 16:4; 6:1-6; 14:23

Coding the Facts Into Pictures or, Symbols in Our Church

part 2 of miniseries
The Church

• KEY CONCEPT

God helped people remember the past and look toward the future by symbolizing facts with things we can see.

• SCRIPTURES

The Passover from Exodus 12, Leviticus 17:11; the Lord's Supper from Mark 14:22-25, Luke 22:14-20, 1 Corinthians 11:23-26.

• GOALS

General: Students will become more aware of symbols and better understand the meanings behind them.
Specific: Students will be able to
A. understand that symbols can help us understand truths
B. translate some common symbols from Scripture
C. explain some common church symbolism

• BACKGROUND

This lesson: Symbols abound in Scripture and church, yet we forget that children do not always understand what they mean. Familiarity does not guarantee comprehension. Perhaps you can remember sometime in your childhood when you were confused by taking literally something that was meant to be symbolic. Adults too may become confused by symbolism. Remember that smart man Nicodemus who thought that to be born again one had to reenter his mother's womb? And closer to this lesson, many turned away from Jesus when He talked about eating His flesh and drinking His blood because they could only think in literal terms rather than in symbols.

To teach an awareness of symbols, and eliminate some of the confusion that it breeds, this lesson uses the Passover celebration and the Lord's Supper to show that by coding important truths into pictures, God helps His people remember what He's done for them and gives them opportunities to pass the information on to their children. You will also have an opportunity to teach your children more about your particular group's symbolism.

For your further study: If you have extra time, consider looking over these resources:
What the Bible Is All About by Henrietta Mears (Regal Books, 1953).
Celebrate the Feasts by Martha Zimmerman (Bethany, 1981).

• PREPARATION

1. Have chalk and a chalkboard available.
2. Cut out the cards from sheet 10-A.

3. Gather a pencil and paper for each child.
4. Pray that God will help your children understand the symbols in His Book and church.
For alternative and optional activities (see below):
Prepare a tray of about 20 common objects and cover them with a kitchen towel.
Cut tagboard for large name tags, and gather paper punch, yarn, scissors, and markers enough for your class.
Set up a communion service or make arrangements for children to attend regular church communion.
Invite your pastor or deacon/elder to talk to your class about the meaning of communion.
Have materials for "Pictionary."

STEP 1

WHAT'S THAT SAY?
Decoding

Write on chalkboard or display on paper: VDKBNLD, BKZRR. **Decipher the coded message by substituting the letter which comes after each letter in the alphabet.** (Z = A, A = B, B = C, etc.) **Raise your hand when you know what the message says.** (Give time for them to solve this.)

Although messages are usually coded to keep people from understanding them, memory experts say that assigning picture images to things can help us remember them.

STEP 2

REPEAT THAT NUMBER
Coding

Write any eight digits on the board. **Look at these numbers for a few seconds and memorize them.** Wait just five seconds, then hide or erase the numbers. **Who can repeat them?** Probably no one will be able to. **Try again using a "coding system."** Write 28175963 on the board. **For this one, visualize 2 people, 8 and 17 years old, counting 59 pennies and 63 dimes.** Discuss whether the "coding" helped and why.

Alternative Approach
Prepare a tray of 20–25 common objects and cover it with a kitchen towel. **After looking at the items on the tray write down as many as you can remember.** Teacher may hold each item up and say what it is: "eraser, safety pin, rubber band," etc. Collect lists after you determine who remembered the most.

Then give some coding hints such as counting the number of objects that start with the letter b, w, etc.; or making a mental picture of the things in some specific place; or creating a silly sentence using the first letter of each object. **Try listing them again. . . . Does coding help you remember?**

OPTIONAL ACTIVITY

Name-Tag Symbols
Have children make name tags, drawing by their name something that symbolizes themselves—something they can do well or plan to learn soon or enjoy doing.

STEP 3

BIBLE CODES
Storytelling

God wants us to remember the good things He's done for us. In the Old Testament one of the ways He helped His people remember was to code those good events into feasts. One such feast was Passover, which is talked about in Exodus 12. It celebrated the greatest event in their history, deliverance from Egypt.

They'd been slaves for over 400 years, twice as long as the United States has been a country! In order to deliver them, God showed His power by sending plagues on the Egyptians. But even when he saw God's power, Pharaoh refused to let them go. Finally God ordered His people to do a peculiar thing. They were to kill a lamb and put its blood across the top and down the sides of their doorposts. Then they roasted the lamb's meat and ate it. That night, in houses where the blood was on the door, the Death Angel passed over. In every home where there was no blood, from Pharaoh down to the least of his servants, the firstborn son died. This great plague convinced Pharaoh to let them leave Egypt.

To remind them of this, God told them to code it into a feast and celebrate it each year. The Passover feast included sacrificing a lamb and eating it. When their children asked why they did these things, they were to answer, "With a mighty hand the Lord brought us out of Egypt, out of the land of slavery."

The night before Jesus was crucified, He ate with His disciples. It was the time of year the Jews were celebrating the Passover, remembering the lambs that died so the people could be delivered from Egypt. After they had eaten, Jesus coded His death, life, and coming again into a ceremony that we call communion or the Lord's Supper to be a reminder of how He came to deliver us from sin. The wine or juice makes us think of His blood, and the bread makes us think of His body being hurt for us so we can be saved and have our sins forgiven.

Can you think of some other symbols or codes believers have used? (Here are some in case you or your kids have trouble thinking of them: a dove stands for the Holy Spirit; incense can stand for prayer—see Revelation 5:8; a fish stands for the Greek letters for Jesus Christ God's Son Savior and was used to show one was a Christian.)

OPTIONAL ACTIVITY

Communion
Have the pastor or deacon/elder explain the communion service. Then if your church allows it, have your children participate with adults, or have a communion service for the class, emphasizing the meaning and symbolism it portrays.

STEP 4

WHAT DOES THIS SYMBOLIZE?
Charades

Play charades using the cards cut from reproducible sheet 10-A. These have some biblical symbols listed.

Close in a prayer that thanks God for giving us "pictures" to help us understand and love Him.

Alternative Approaches
Have students make extra cards on other biblical and/or church symbols. If your church has more symbolism in its worship, you will especially want to use this approach.

Play a game like Pictionary instead with these cards in which you give the "artist" the name of what is symbolized and he draws the church's symbol for those trying to guess what he was told to draw.

IDEAS FOR EXPANDING THIS LESSON

Start a class notebook or chart of biblical symbols. Write them down each time you find one in a lesson and have children bring them from their own study or reading.

Encourage children to start a personal notebook of biblical symbols. Have them bring them back to class and share what they've found.

Research the Christian meaning behind the common symbols of Christmas or Easter.

Use the Charades/Pictionary game in Step 4 throughout the year as a sponge activity to keep them aware of symbols and their meanings and usefulness.

Encourage children to code a family experience into a special meal so that they can remember what God did for them.

You could also plan a meal as a group that reminds them of what God has done. Before or after the meal you could use some of the above activities, such as the game or notebooks.

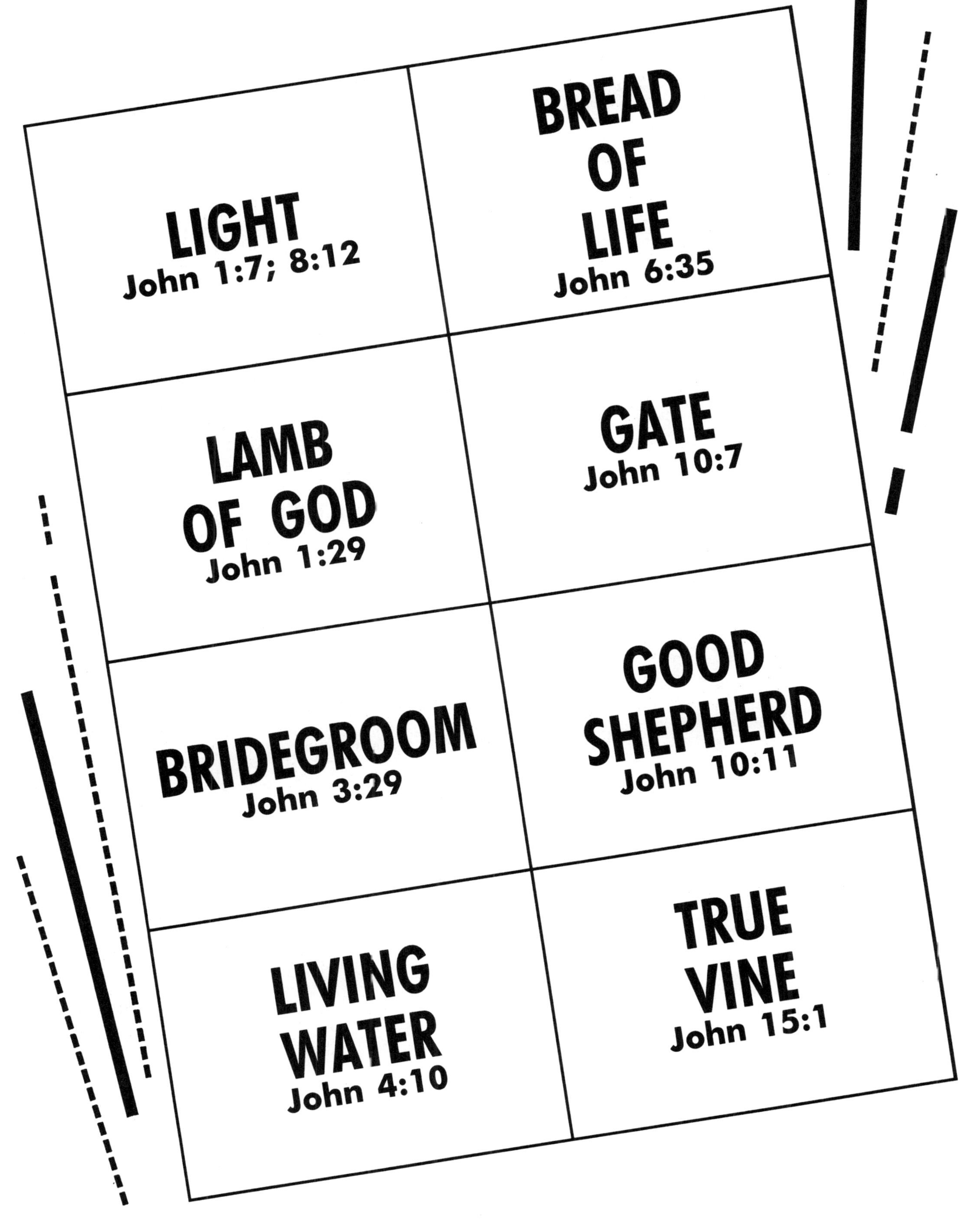
LIGHT
John 1:7; 8:12
BREAD OF LIFE
John 6:35
LAMB OF GOD
John 1:29
GATE
John 10:7
BRIDEGROOM
John 3:29
GOOD SHEPHERD
John 10:11
LIVING WATER
John 4:10
TRUE VINE
John 15:1

The Next-Greatest Story Ever Told or, The Church Through History

part 3 of miniseries The Church

• KEY CONCEPT God has given His church a fascinating history through the centuries.

• SCRIPTURES Matthew 16:18; Acts 1:8

• GOALS

General: Each student will have a sense of the flow of the church's history since Acts.

Specific: Students will be able to

A. recount some of the major happenings in the church since Acts
B. appreciate that although God has given people different levels of understanding of His truth, He has always had people in history who loved Him
C. understand that even in the midst of persecution God was loving His children

• BACKGROUND

This lesson: History has the word *story* in it, but sometimes we forget that.

Your kids won't forget it about church history, though, after this meeting. They'll take part in a grand production that summarizes things God has done through His people since the time of the New Testament. Then they'll play a game to help each other remember the story even better.

May this be the beginning of a love affair with God's wonderful stories about His people, and may you and your kids be inspired to "make history" yourselves.

For your further study: If you have extra time, consider looking over these resources.

Sketches from Church History by S.M. Houghton (Banner of Truth, 1980) tells church history like the story it is, and has interesting historical paintings and other illustrations.

An Almanac of the Christian Church by William D. Blake (Bethany, 1987) lists fascinating and important happenings in church history for all the days of the year.

The New International Dictionary of the Christian Church edited by J.D. Douglas (Zondervan, 1978) is a respected quick-reference guide for more details on the people and places and events of church history.

"Saints" by William Barton (Woodside Music, P.O. Box 620-400, Woodside, CA 94062) is a delightful audiocassette of original ballads about heroes in church history. Some of them are possibly from a different church background than yours, but you should be able to use many of the songs. You could plug them into the script below; for example, "The Martyrs of Sebastea" tells the dramatic story of the martyrdom of 30 Christian Roman soldiers and would fit in the script beginning with "Many Roman emperors did things like this." Dr. Barton also travels and does concerts on this theme; you may contact him at the above address.

• PREPARATION

1. Gather enough Bibles for every kid to have one.
2. Make photocopies of reproducible sheet 11-A, enough for every kid to have one and tear out reproducible sheets 11-B and C.
3. Gather two papers and pencils.
For alternative and optional activities (see below):
Do research on what additional things you'd like to teach about church history.
Gather costumes, sets, etc. for a more dramatic production.
Gather books on church history.
Gather materials to make board games.
Gather materials to make calendars.

STEP 1

ACT ME OUT A STORY
The Production

Hand out reproducible sheet 11-A to everyone. Assign one student the part of John Huss. Give five students reproducible sheets 11-B and -C and have them divide up the reading. Then go right into the following script that incorporates dramatic readings, narration, and worship . . .

It was the last half of the first century, about 70 years after Jesus was born. Most of the New Testament was already written.

The church, God's people, was growing. Not because it was exactly a nice group to be a part of—I mean, it was dangerous to be a Christian then. In fact, I think you'll agree after this meeting that it usually has been dangerous to be a Christian.

For example, around A.D. 64 (explain if necessary that A.D. stands for Anno Domini, "The year of the Lord" in Latin, and means it's about that many years after Jesus was born; B.C. stands for "Before Christ"), **there was a bad fire in the city of Rome. Rome was the capital city of one of the most important groups of nations in history, called the Roman Empire. The head of the Roman Empire then, the emperor, was Nero. He decided to blame the Christians for starting the fire! Lots of people believe Nero set the fire himself!**

And Nero didn't just blame them; he had them killed. And he didn't just have them killed; he had them tortured and killed in awful ways like burning and being eaten by dogs and being crucified.

Many Roman emperors did things like this to the Christians. It's called "persecution." In fact, thousands of Christians died, and the persecution lasted for over 200 years.

Then something happened in A.D. 311 A man named Constantine became the emperor. There's a story that he saw in the sky a cross on fire with words written on it that said, "By this, conquer." That was just

before an important battle which he won. After that Constantine not only stopped any persecution of Christians, but he gave Christians great honor. Christians got the leadership jobs in the empire. The church became very rich.

Sounds like a very nice change, huh? Well, it certainly was. But can anyone think of any dangers that could come? Let them guess.

Some people said they were Christians just so they could get the better jobs, and they didn't know Jesus. And then Constantine decided he would be the leader of the church, and didn't seem to remember that Jesus is the only King of the church. Eventually men called popes felt they could tell the church and countries what to do. A lot of people started teaching things that did not agree with the Bible.

There was one big meeting around then at a place called Nicea that came up with a paper that a lot of people read in churches even today. It's called the Nicene Creed, and it was written because some people were teaching that Jesus is not God. Have your students read the creed together out loud from their sheet 11-A. You may need to explain that *Catholic* means "universal," referring to the whole church.

There were several church leaders who helped people learn what God said about important things in the Bible. Some famous ones were Ambrose and Augustine and Jerome.

Something else happened around then when people saw the problems coming into the church that seemed worse than being persecuted. Some people felt they could please God by getting into small groups and living away from the rest of the world. This is called the beginning of monasticism. Many monks and nuns from this type of living helped keep books that would have been lost, and they helped the poor and sick.

Meanwhile a big religion was getting started called Islam. Its followers even created a larger empire than the Roman Empire, called the Mohammedan or Muslim Empire. One of its leaders, Caliph Omar, destroyed the world's most famous library because he felt the Muslim "Bible" called the Koran was the only book needed in the world! Thousands of Christian churches were destroyed or made into mosques, where Muslims worship their god Allah. This is still a very big religion in the world.

Meanwhile more was going on in the church. Back then England was a pretty wild place, and missionaries went to it and told people about Jesus. Some of the most famous were Boniface and Patrick—ever hear of St. Patrick's Day? That's the guy!

Anyway, back to the Moslems. How many of you heard of knights? Well, hundreds of knights and thousands of soldiers went on the Crusades. There were fierce people known as the Turks who took over the land where Jesus used to live, called the Holy Land by many Christians. The Turks became Muslims, and they started hurting Christians who tried to visit where Jesus used to live. So, many soldiers were sent on the Crusades to try to get the land back in friendly hands. These took place over hundreds of years! One of the Crusades is a terribly sad story. It's called the Children's Crusade. Want to hear about it? (We assume your kids will!)

There was a boy named Stephen in France who said that Jesus had

appeared to him and told him that he would help children do what so many soldiers and kings had not been able to do. He said that if a lot of kids stood by a sea in France, the water would part before them like it did for Moses. Then they could walk over to the Holy Land. A boy in Germany, named Nicholas, told other kids. And I mean a *lot* of other kids. Thousands of kids, boys and girls, the average age 12, started to march to meet by the sea in France. As they marched they sang a song that I think is a lot like one you might know. Of course, they sang it in another language. Let's sing it now. Sing the verse of "Fairest Lord Jesus" provided on reproducible sheet 11-A. **You may have heard of the Alps. They're beautiful but dangerous mountains in Europe, mountains that have snow on them all year round. The kids had to cross them. And many of them died.**

But a lot of them made it to the sea and met the kids from France. Of course the sea did not open up before them, though.

What could they do? Many turned around and went home. But 5,000 stayed. Seven ships offered to take them to the Holy Land, and they got on.

Two of the ships ran into rocks, though, and sank. And something worse, maybe, happened to the kids on the other five ships—the captains turned out to be slave-dealers, and they sold the children to Muslims! They never saw their homes again.

Well, a lot of things were happening in the world then, so many we'd be here all day and night and still not get through the story. But let me simplify it a bit and tell you that the church for the most part was getting farther away from what Jesus taught. It even taught that if you served the church you could get forgiveness for sins, and even if you just paid money you could get forgiven! People who tried to teach against the church got into trouble.

Of course God still cared for His church, though. Something exciting began to happen that's called the Reformation today, something that helped people learn again how to really get to heaven. Many of its followers were called Protestants. There were people called the Waldenians and men like one named John Wycliffe who helped people learn what the Bible said. Wycliffe even translated the Bible into the people's language. Copies had to be made by hand; there were still no printing presses. This is in the 1300s, over 600 years ago. John Huss is another famous person from this time. He preached about Jesus in the city of Prague, which made many of the church leaders angry. His books were burned in the courtyard of the archbishop's palace. John Huss was asked if he would obey the commands of the pope. This is what John Huss said: have the child with the part of John Huss read part one of his script.

Huss was not allowed by the pope to teach in the church anymore. He even had the whole city punished until Huss left. But eventually Huss was arrested and placed in a dungeon next to the city sewer! He was brought to trial. The sentence was passed: John Huss and his books were to be burned! Huss kneeled down before everyone and prayed out loud: have the child read part two of his script.

John Huss was led out to die. The priests cried out, "We commit your

soul to the devil!" John Huss answered, have child read part three. **Then over and over Huss cried,** have child read part four. **The wood and straw were piled up around him even as he still spoke . . . and soon his body was dead.**

There were so many other heroes I don't have time to tell you about now. Like Savonarola and Erasmus and Zwingli and Calvin. Let me tell you about two heroes, though, one a group of people and the other a very famous man.

Have your five narrators read the story of Martin Luther from sheets 11-B and -C. If you wish, sing one verse of "A Mighty Fortress Is Our God."

In France, Protestants were called Huguenots. They actually fought religious wars in France for 30 years, against people who did not believe the Bible! The queen mother of France in the late 1500s was Catherine de Medici. She said that it was too bad that the wars were going on, and she said she had a great idea to get a treaty set. She invited all the "important people" of the land to a wedding. The people came and the wedding took place.

Everybody was celebrating. It was evening. Queen-Mother Catherine went to her son, the king, and told him that the Huguenots had formed a plot to kill the entire royal family and the leaders of the Catholics! The king signed a paper that said anyone who wanted to in Paris could kill the Huguenots! The mob went wild; soon thousands of Huguenots were dead.

But guess what? Most of those who were not killed escaped to other countries, and the Huguenots had been among the smartest and most skilled workers in the entire country of France. A famous writer said that the French leaders had ruined their country in the name of religion.

There were more battles and wars, I'm sorry to say. One of the most famous is called the Thirty Years' War in Germany, fought in the 1600s.

Remember how I mentioned England got missionaries when it was wild? Well, by the 1500s England was pretty Christian. But then there was a group called Puritans that felt there had not been enough change for the better. Eventually there were wars in the country over it. Have you ever heard of the story of Pilgrim's Progress? It was written by John Bunyan, who was put in jail for years for preaching without the government's permission! In fact, he wrote it in jail.

I've not said much about Canada or the United States, have I? Nothing, in fact. This was still a hundred years before America became an independent nation. Many Puritans helped settle America.

Well, even after all those battles and all those sermons, the Protestant church still had problems. Not with the Catholics, but with itself so there were many people who taught others how they felt they should get to know God better.

There came a time when a lot of Christians in America and England changed a lot, to try to follow God better. Some famous preachers were Jonathan Edwards, John Wesley, and George Whitefield.

I've really not said much about Africa or South America either, have I? Or China and other places. It's because, I'm sorry to say, very, very few Christians ever got there. Finally, in the late 1700s, which was

after America was an independent nation, people began to be more interested in helping others know about Jesus in those other countries. Some famous missionaries were William Carey to India, Adoniram Judson to Burma, Robert and Mary Moffat to Africa, James Hudson Taylor to China, and John Paton to the New Hebrides islands. As John Paton was getting ready to leave, he was told by an old man in Scotland, "But the cannibals! You will be eaten by the cannibals!" But he wasn't, and then so many people became Christians that he said "his joy was almost too great to be borne."

So many more things happened, of course, too. The Sunday School a lot like we know it became common for the first time in the 1800s. In the 1900s there were countries taken over by people who did not allow the church to meet, and many Christians were killed and are still being killed. In the free countries many books began to be published which are still being published on hundreds of things about the Bible.

Christians still don't agree on everything, by any means. God doesn't even say we have to agree on everything. But He's always had people who truly love Him and their neighbor and try to obey what He has given us in the Bible. And even when those people were *killed* **because they loved God, God took care of them and carried them home to heaven. God's enemies cannot stop His church.** Have everyone read Matthew 16:18 from reproducible sheet 11-A.

Let's all pray and thank God for the wonderful heroes and heroines He has given us in church history, and let's pray that we would be faithful like they were . . .

STEP 2

WHAT WAS THAT POINT?
Game

Divide your class into two groups and give them each a paper and pencil. They are to make up and write down questions about church history to ask the other group when it is their turn. Let them look at this book if they need to.

Alternative Approaches
You may wish to gather other church history books for your kids to make up "bonus questions" for the other group on parts of church history not covered in this lesson. Have them briefly summarize for the other group what they learned from their other books before the game begins, so the other group has a chance at answering these additional questions correctly.

Let your class, if you have time and the materials, instead make up board games about church history.

OPTIONAL ACTIVITY

Making Calendars
Have your kids design and make a twelve-month-or-less calendar labeled with interesting dates in church history. Use as your reference a book such as *An Almanac of the Christian Church* listed in the above resources.

IDEAS FOR EXPANDING THIS LESSON

Please see the suggestions just before this lesson for using lessons 9–11 in a series on the church. It includes having a production for other people and winding up with some clever refreshments.

NICENE CREED

I believe in one God, the Father Almighty, Maker of heaven and earth, and of all things visible and invisible.

And in one Lord Jesus Christ, the only-begotten Son of God, begotten of the Father before all worlds; God of God, Light of Light, very God of very God; begotten, not made, being of one substance with the Father, by whom all things were made.

Who, for us men and for our salvation, came down from heaven, and was incarnate by the Holy Spirit of the Virgin Mary, and was made man; and was crucified also for us under Pontius Pilate; He suffered and was buried; and the third day He rose again, according to the Scriptures; and ascended into heaven, and sitteth on the right hand of the Father; and He shall come again, with glory, to judge the living and the dead; whose kingdom shall have no end.

And I believe in the Holy Spirit, the Lord and Giver of life; who proceedeth from the Father and the Son; who with the Father and the Son together is worshiped and glorified; who spake by the prophets.

And I believe in one holy catholic and apostolic church. I acknowledge one baptism for the remission of sins; and I look for the resurrection of the dead, and the life of the world to come. AMEN.

Fair are the meadows,
Fairer still the woodlands,
Robed in the pleasant garb of spring;
Jesus is fairer, Jesus is purer,
He makes the grieving heart to sing.

Jesus said,
"I will build My church,
and the gates of hell
will not overcome it."
Matthew 16:18

You are John Huss.

Part one: Yes, so far as they agree with the doctrine of Christ—but when I see the contrary I will not obey them, even though you burn my body.

Part two: Lord Jesus, pardon all my enemies for the sake of Your great mercy. You know that they have falsely accused me, brought forward false witnesses, and concocted false charges against me. Pardon them for the sake of Your infinite mercy.

Part three: And I commit it to the Lord Jesus Christ!

Part four: Into Your hands, O Lord, I commend my spirit. I am willing patiently and publicly to endure this dreadful, shameful, and cruel death for the sake of Your Gospel and the preaching of Your Word.

MARTIN LUTHER

Who was this man who vowed to become a monk because he was almost struck by a bolt of lightning? —who beat himself unconscious to try to atone for his sin? —who spent hours at confession, who cried in despair, "Oh, my sins! my sins!" —who is called "the man who rediscovered God's grace"?

Martin Luther. Gloriously saved, gladly telling the world the "rediscovered" truth of the Gospel.

The world of his time, that is. He was nine years old when Christopher Columbus sailed to America. He was born November 10, 1483, in Eisleben, Germany.

He became a Roman Catholic monk at 22.

To gain salvation he sacrificed everything. Once for two weeks he ate nothing, drank nothing, and did not sleep. Still peace did not come to him.

He did not then understand Paul's words in Romans that the Gospel is the saving power of God to everyone who believes in Christ, *because* it reveals the righteousness of God. God rightly justifies us because Christ suffered in our place and Christ is righteous.

When the Holy Spirit revealed this to Martin Luther, he said that "the light of the truth shone with such brilliance, and brought such deliverance to my soul, that I felt the words 'The just shall live by faith' were the very gates of Paradise itself." The Bible became to him a book of life and comfort.

Luther went to Rome. He was not yet a Reformer, trying to change the church. On seeing Rome from a distance, he fell upon his knees and cried, "Hail, holy Rome, thrice holy for the blood of martyrs shed here." But at the end of his visit, he was prepared to say, "If there is a hell, Rome is built over it . . . (But) I would not have missed seeing Rome for 100,000 florins. I should have felt always an uneasy doubt whether I was not, after all, doing injustice to the Pope. As it is, I am quite satisfied on the point."

Yet still he did not raise a strong protest against the church. Until—John Tetzel—fat, greasy-vested, and eloquent, sent by the Pope to sell indulgences. And also a slow-witted farmer from Martin's own parish.

"This here paper's going to send my old mother—God love 'er soul—right up to heaven," confided the lumbering old peasant, catching up with Martin on the road outside of Wittenberg one night in 1517. "Right out of purgatory it's going to take the dear saint," he added, waving a dirty piece of paper in Martin's face.

"Where'd you get that?" Martin asked roughly. The farmer was clutching an indulgence—a greasy paper, to be sure—but Martin knew that the peasant had paid a week's wages for it, and that he had been sold a dozen fantastic promises with it. "Where'd you get that?"

"From Tetzel," the farmer told him.

"But he's under oath not to sell his indulgences in Wittenberg!"

"He didn't," the farmer said slyly. "I crossed the river to buy 'em. We all did. 'Twas worth the trip. 'When the coin in the coffer rings, the soul from purgatory springs!' That's what Tetzel says, Doctor Luther."

Anyone listening at the door of Martin's room that night could have heard his quill scratching restlessly on parchment. Finally, he threw the quill down, strode from the room. The moon lit the

way to the door of the Castle Church. And the sound of pounding rattled through the night, as Martin Luther tacked up his parchment. This was the 95 Theses. It was October 31, 1517.

"Indulgences," he said, "are simply remissions of penalties which the church on earth has imposed. They have no effect on the souls of the departed, and they don't remit sin in heaven; only God can do that."

The Pope called Luther "a child of the devil." Luther said the Pope was Antichrist.

As you can tell, the Reformation was well and truly under way. "A single man had risen in revolt against the religious ideas of Church and State, and all the forces of Church and State were invoked to quell him. Henry VIII, king of England, was himself engaged in writing a book against Luther." Luther had been called to appear at Worms, where 206 persons of rank stood to oppose him. He spent much of the night in prayer:

"O God, my God, be with me and protect me against my enemies of the world. Thou must do it, for in me is no strength. It is Thy cause, O God, not mine."

Perhaps you have heard what Luther said the next day in reply to the question of whether he would recant—it was "the speech that shook the world." First he said it in Latin, then in German. It ended thus:

"Unless I am convinced by testimonies of the Scriptures or by clear arguments that I am in error . . . I cannot withdraw, for I am subject to the Scriptures I have quoted; my conscience is captive to the Word of God. It is unsafe and dangerous to do anything against one's conscience. Here I stand; I cannot do otherwise. So help me God."

Luther was placed under the ban of the Empire. Anyone who gave him lodging, food, or drink was to be charged with high treason against the Emperor. He dressed up as a knight and hid in a castle for a while.

But God protected him for many years. He married a former nun, Catherine Von Bora. They had six children. Luther said that parents should be the mirrors of God's grace to their children. Luther described the mother of his children as his "pious, faithful, and devoted wife, always loving, worthy, and beautiful."

She was indeed a domestic reformer to Luther—his friend Melancthon tells us that in earlier times Luther's bed had not been made for a whole year—he was too busy to make it!

Luther remained a busy man to the end of his life. To copy his written works would take a rapid writer an average lifetime if he worked at the rate of 10 hours a day. His works include hymns, and he has been called "the father of congregational song."

His most famous hymn is EIN FESTE BURG, "A Mighty Fortress Is Our God." It is considered the battle-song of the Reformation. In his life on earth, which ended in 1546, Martin Luther lived the truth of his words,

"And though this world, with devils
filled, should threaten to undo us,
We will not fear, for God hath willed
His truth to triumph through us."

The truth?—"the just shall live by faith alone"—by God's matchless grace.

Body Builders
or, Physical Appearance

- **KEY CONCEPT**

God made our bodies and wants us to keep them in good shape.

- **SCRIPTURES**

Psalm 139:13-16; 2 Corinthians 6:16; 2 Timothy 1:14; Proverbs 31:30; 1 Samuel 16:7; 1 Peter 3:3-4; Philippians 1:20; 3:20-21

- **GOALS**

General: The students will affirm good things about their bodies and discover ways to improve them.
Specific: Students will be able to
A. identify what they like about their bodies and ways they can improve them
B. discover that God made them the way they are and lives in them
C. select one way to improve their bodies this week

- **BACKGROUND**

This lesson: God says our bodies are important. After all, He designed them and lives in them! At the same time, we are not to let our physical appearance detract from a godly character. Finding the balance can be tricky.

Like adults, kids vary widely on how they view their bodies. Some are very negative, hating the way they look. Others are beginning to spend too much time on their physical appearance in order to fit in or to attract attention. As you plan this lesson, think about how each student in your group views his body and what kinds of improvements he needs to make in order to make it a fit living place for God. Then tailor the activities to fit the needs of your students.

For your further study: If you have extra time, consider looking over these resources.

Family Fitness Fun by Dr. Charles T. Kuntzleman (Here's Life Publishers, 1990).

What's a Body to Do? by Ruth Shannon Odor (Standard Publishing Co., 1980). Although this book is written for younger kids, it gives helpful information that can be used in the suggested learning centers.

- **PREPARATION**

1. Gather marking pens, scissors, masking tape, paper, and Bibles—enough for every student.
2. Bring magazines and/or newspapers that include ads for body-care products.

3. Pray that your kids will accept their bodies and want to care for them.

For alternative and optional activities (see below):

Cut three body shapes out of poster board. With a black marking pen, print in large letters one of the following sentences on separate shapes: (1) God made you the way you are. (2) There are some things about your body that you can change. (3) God lives in you.

Record on video or audio tape several TV or radio commercials for body-care products. Have the necessary equipment available for playing the tape in class.

Ask qualified people (e.g., doctor, nurse, health teacher, beautician) to conduct one of the following learning center activities: Exercise/Sports; Nutrition, Hygiene, Sleep; Substance Abuse; Hairstyles and Fashion for boys and girls separately. Have the leader plan about 10 minutes of information and/or activity. Include as many centers as you can, depending on time and available personnel. Don't overlook knowledgeable people even though they may not be considered experts.

STEP 1

A GREAT BODY
Advertisements

Have kids locate ads for body care in magazines and/or newspapers. Discuss: **What do these ads tell us?**

Say: **Advertisers try to convince us that their products will make our bodies more appealing and will give us instant popularity. But God gives us different messages in His Word.**

Alternative Approach

Instead of showing print ads, play TV or radio commercials that you recorded.

STEP 2

LOOKING AT OUR BODIES
Art

Say: **Before we discover what God says about our bodies, let's take a look at ours.** Give everyone paper, marking pen, and scissors. Have students draw a picture of themselves, leaving room to write a few words on the pictures.

Have everyone write on his trunk what he likes about his body, such as eyes to see, able to walk, can hug. After a few minutes, have everyone write on the arms and legs what he doesn't like about his body. Then have them place a check in front of the disliked features that cannot be changed, such as height.

Point out that we all have features and abilities that we like and dislike. But like it or not, this is the body God gave each one of us.

STEP 3

GOD AND OUR BODIES
Scripture

Say: **There are three important facts about our bodies that we need to know and remember. The first one is found in Psalm 139:13-16.** Have students turn to this passage, and ask a volunteer to read it aloud. Say, **God made us the way we are. Even before we were born, He decided how**

tall we would be, what color eyes and hair we would have, what we would look like. We may not agree with how God made us, but He didn't make any mistakes.

Then remark, **There are some things about our bodies that we can change, however.** Ask students to name some of these (e.g., weight, hair style). **Even though we can't change our height, for example, we can dress in ways that will make us look taller. God gives us the "basics" to work with, and we can help our bodies look good.**

The third fact about our bodies is found in 2 Corinthians 6:16 and 2 Timothy 1:14. Ask two volunteers to read these verses aloud. Say, **If we have put our faith in God, He lives in our bodies in the Person of the Holy Spirit. Consequently, He wants us to keep our bodies healthy and free from harmful things such as drugs.**

OPTIONAL ACTIVITY

Learning Centers

Say: **There are some practical things we can do to keep our bodies in shape and to help us look our best for God.** Direct the kids' attention to the learning centers you set up before class, briefly explaining what each one is about. Divide your students into the same number of groups as centers, and direct each group to a leader. After a set time, have the groups rotate to a new center. Or let everyone choose which center they want to go to and move to another one when ready.

STEP 4

HOW IMPORTANT IS THIS?

Bible Study

Say: **We need to take care of our bodies, but some people put too much emphasis on them. Let's take a closer look at God's perspective on our physical appearance.** One at a time, have two students look up the following verses and summarize what they say about our physical appearance.

- Proverbs 31:30.
- 1 Samuel 16:7.
- 1 Peter 3:3-4.
- Philippians 1:20—Discuss: **How can we use our bodies to bring praise to God?**
- Philippians 3:20-21.

Point out that we need to find a balance between taking care of our bodies and growing spiritually. We can't do just one or the other and be the kind of person God wants us to be.

STEP 5

IMPROVING MY BODY

Decisions

Until we get our new bodies, let's think about what we can do to improve the ones we have without spending a ridiculous amount of

time on our physical appearance. Direct students to look at the pictures they drew earlier. Have them decide on one thing they will begin to do this week to improve their bodies, and write it on the head.

STEP 6

HELP ME, GOD
Prayer

Have students pray silently, thanking God for their bodies and asking Him to help them begin the chosen improvement this week. Close with audible prayer.

Have everyone take their body pictures home. Encourage students to post them in their rooms, perhaps on a closet door.

IDEAS FOR EXPANDING THIS LESSON

Plan a body-building day when your students can expand the time spent at the learning centers. For example, complete a kids' exercise video, spend more time experimenting with hairstyles, try on clothes to discover what colors and styles look best. Start or end with a healthy meal.

Go out to eat together, and give prizes to the people who eat the healthiest meals.

Spend an afternoon playing sports games for exercise.

Super Meetings for Kids
Did It Work?

DEAR LEADER,

You can have a real impact on future Kid Builder products! Please take a minute to fill out this form, giving us your candid reaction to this material. Thanks for your help.

About You

In what setting(s) did you use these lessons? (Sunday School, youth group, midweek Bible study, etc.)

How many kids were in your group?

What was the age-range of those in your group?

Did you use all or some of these lessons? If "some," which ones did you use?

How long was your average meeting time?

(Optional) Name
Address

☐ If you are interested in helping write future Kid Builders products, check here and be sure to fill in the above name and address.

About This Book

Did you and your children enjoy this study? Why or why not?

What are the strengths and weaknesses of this book?

About the Future

What would you like to see covered in future Kid Builder books?

Do you plan to use other Kid Builder books? Why or why not?

Do you plan to repeat any of these sessions in the future with new students? Why or why not?

PLACE
STAMP
HERE

Victor Books
Kid Builders Editor
1825 College Avenue
Wheaton, Illinois 60187